Werner Herzog • Screenplays

Werner Herzog

Screenplays

Aguirre, the Wrath of God
Every Man for Himself and God Against All
Land of Silence and Darkness

Translated from the German by
Alan Greenberg and Martje Herzog

TANAM PRESS • NEW YORK • 1980

Translation © 1980 by Tanam Press
Originally published in German as
DREHBÜCHER II, © 1979 Carl Hanser Verlag
All rights reserved
First American edition, 1980
Printed in the United States of America
ISBN 0-934378-02-9 (cloth)
ISB N 0-934378-03-7 (paper)

Rear cover photograph by Alan Greenberg

The texts in this volume have remained completely unchanged, in the shape they were before
shooting started. The films themselves, as one
can see, followed a very different evolution.

For "Land of Silence and Darkness", there was
no screenplay. The film has but one element, Fini
Straubinger, the principal character. So in this
case, there is a transcript of the spoken dialogue
from the film.

This volume is dedicated to Fini Staubinger.

Munich, 8/7/77   W.H.

Aguirre, the Wrath of God

Characters:

Gonzalo Pizarro, brother of Francisco Pizarro
Lope de Aguirre, "The Wrath of God"
Pedro de Ursua, a Spanish nobleman
Inez de Atienza, Ursua's mistress
Fernando de Guzman, "Emperor of Peru"
Flores, daughter of Aguirre
Juan de Analte, young Hidalgo
Gaspar de Carvajal, a Dominican monk
Chimalpahin, an Indian nobleman, called
   Baltasar
Diego Bermudez
Sebastian de Fuenterrabia } confidants of
Gustavo Perucho   } Aguirre

Description of the Characters

Gonzalo Pizarro:
> tall, incredibly lean, his cheeks suggesting that he suffers from some disease of the stomach. Unscrupulous and, like his brother Francisco Pizarro, the typical highly-intelligent illiterate.

Lope de Aguirre:
> he calls himself either "The Great Betrayer" or "The Wrath of God". Fanatical, possessed, and with limitless ambition, but extremely methodical in his actions. There is a likeness between his type and late photographs of Kafka, with a black glimmer in the eyes. About forty years of age, taciturn, sinewy, and with hands like clutching steel claws. "Hands," Aguirre once said, "are made to clutch and grasp." Unscrupulous, and with an almost pathological criminal energy, yet so utterly human that one could not say, this kind of man no longer exists.

Pedro de Ursua:
> a little younger than Aguirre but of a more ancient nobility and, like him, a Basque. Ursua is built strongly, tending somewhat towards corpulence. His greasy face is a bit fleshy, with perceivable shadows from his beard, and constantly seems to betray a sallow and sickly pallor. Physically and mentally very strong, with nimble somewhat uncontrolled movements.

Inez de Atienza:

> between twenty-five and thirty, noble, giving the faint impression of a madonna. Self-composed, never losing her dignity even in the greatest misery. Unobtrusive and very devoted.

Fernando de Guzman:

> an officer to whom no one paid any attention until, suddenly, through the machinations of Aguirre, he is proclaimed Emperor of Peru. Relatively colorless, of mediocre intelligence and, in comparison to the others, rather restrained in his craving for gold. Guzman is the eldest of the expedition, and his hair and beard already show streaks of white. Strongly boned horse-like face. After his promotion, develops a naive vanity.

Flores, daughter of Aguirre:

> Thirteen years old, just released from the convent, flowering into a beauty. She is Innocence and, together with Arnalte, personifies a kind of hope in the film. Still almost childlike, like a birch. Her breasts are still small.

Juan de Arnalte:

> still makes the impression of an adolescent Hidalgo. Typical of the sentimental youth, the youthful lover. Even when wounded, he is still graceful. Often fighting an inner battle between military obedience and human impulse.

Gaspar de Carvajal:

> Dominican monk, in frock and with tonsure; later on his hair grows carelessly and gets

woolly. Rather young yet, and almost rabidly fanatical in converting people. Somewhat like Artaud in the film of Jeanne d'Arc by Dreyer.

Chimalpahin:

Indian noble, called Baltasar. Not yet thirty years old, slender with tawny complexion. Noble features, long blue-black hair, very graceful movements despite his handcuffs. Very dignified, and makes an impression of deep resignation. Continually wrapped in profound silence and almost apathetic, his gaze directed far off into the distance, dozing.

Diego Bermudez:

is appointed scrivener. Nimble, cynical, and loyal to crime alone. Versed in expressing himself.

Sebastian de Fuenterrabia and Gustavo Perucho:

scoundrels craving for gold, depraved and violent, at first glance recognizable as "villains". Perucho wants only to give the defenseless Indians "a piece of my mind", and Fuenterrabia boasts: "I don't booze, I don't battle, I don't whore. My only vice is hunting Indians...."

March through the Andes

There are snowy peaks all around, majestic crests, and the mountains tower like Holy Cathedrals. Very clear, icy, silent air, frost lying on the hoary ground, all in deep, majestic silence. From the mountain crests, glacial tongues lick down into the depths. Clouds are gathering around the crests, as if coming out of nowhere. The air further above is light and blue, deep down it is a deep purple. Nothing at all is stirring. The huge mountains tower one above the other up to 18,000 feet, in profound silence.

All at once, there, in a breathtaking sweep, and with a breathtaking zoom that makes you dizzy, the camera picks out the top of a pass: now, suddenly, we recognize a thin thread of people there in zigzag formation, and we can distinguish hardly any movement. At certain points the thread is broken, then followed up again, winding through rocks, slag, and ice. The dizzying gaze still moves downward into the deep: we realize now that there are hundreds, dragging themselves along, hundreds, one man after another. Animals are now distinctly recognizable, some horses, llamas and, on the glacier, some pigs. They are standing in a long line at the edge of a crevice exhausted to death. The file works its way forward with great effort.

Now we are close to them: There are bearded Spaniards in armor bearing swords, and all of them can hardly hold out any longer. Some carry arquebuses and gunpowder, some drag horses

along by the bridle, and—almost unbelievably—there are Indians carrying two sedan
chairs. Then a long, listless line of Indians with
long blue-black hair. They are wearing ponchos
and knitted-wool caps with ear flaps. They are
bound to each other by chains in a ghastly
fashion. Spaniards with crossbows beside them,
and further down, Indians again, dragging a cannon with heavy wheels, they are half-dead. Thirty
Indians drag the cannon with ropes.

Fog gathers around the slopes, enveloping the
thread and setting it free again. In the distance,
woolly clouds are swelling. No one utters a
sound, no one utters a single word, only deep,
heavy breathing and panting. A line of panting
llamas bogs down, all of them carry heavy
burdens. They are gasping and snorting, perturbed, some are sniffing and wrinkling their velvety
nostrils.

A Spaniard is poking a pig on the glacier, but the
pig doesn't stir. Everything is a unique unheard-
of effort. The pigs are completely done in.

Now we behold a Spaniard whose nose begins to
bleed from thin air and exhaustion, but he is so
exhausted that he doesn't even wipe himself.
From higher up loose stones come rumbling
down upon the people, the stones making a
rumbling, hollow noise.

Suddenly, a call heard from above spreads from
one man to another; getting louder, it becomes
intelligible, passes on, sinks down and disappears
into the deep. ''We've made it!'' they are
shouting and: ''Here we are, at the top!'' But
there are no signs of joy, no one moves faster or

quickens his pace. The call resounds in the depths, as if no one understood it, as if it were nothing to no one.

Only up on the pass, where there is a pile of stones with flags of faded fabric flapping on it, everything starts to move a bit, then the order of the march is disturbed and comes to a halt. The men drop to their knees, and the Indians, bound to each other by their chains, relieve themselves of their burdens, drop to their knees, and with hands folded in front of their mouths, fervently pray.

Now we recognize Carvajal, the Dominican monk; he takes his crucifix from his chest, his left hand extending it far out over the land, beyond the pass, and blesses it with his right hand. And now we also catch sight of Aguirre, whose face is marked by the ascent and his unlimited willpower. "We've made it," a man beside him weeps. "Men," says Aguirre, "that was merely one step."

March atop the high plateau

A vast elevated plain framed by gigantic mountains, the march proceeds. A strong wind blows driving sand before it, the animals huddle close to each other. Nothing but a scant few, very hard tufts of grass grow at this height, with white streaks of saltpeter amongst them. Clouds are towering one above the other.

Now we see a flock of wild alpacas whose fur is being tousled by the wind. They are standing still, noses twitching, full of distrust, then suddenly, the whole flock flees, clustering closely to each other, dust swirling up behind them.

The file of Spaniards, closer. Strong as the clouds, the army marches on. A sedan-chair is carried along, the Indian bearers carry it in their customary quick-paced trot, with the other sedan behind them. Flores pushes the curtain aside a little and looks out, as the sedan has been forced to stop because of some timid llamas. Laden llamas behind the sedan, then Indians, neglected and linked to each other, Spaniards amongst them, armored and carrying heavy weaponry, pigs and then, more Spaniards. Roughly, they are pushing the Indians onward.

The vanguard. Gonzalo Pizarro, riding a nervous horse; he is harnessed and wears a flying cape, lanky and unbelievably lean, giving an impression of intelligence at first glance. Beside him, Ursua, somewhat insignificant, of average stature. His fleshy face has a pale ashen tint. Ursua gives a rather unhealthy impression, sickly but still quite agile and full of energy. Trailing those two, some soldiers—wild-looking sorts, filthy—and we know at once that they are ready to do anything at any time. The Indians, in spite of their rags — some wear shirts and trousers, many are barefoot or have sandals that are far too flimsy — leave a much cleaner impression. They are plodding on in deep apathetic resignation, scarcely paying attention along the way. They are so sure of their mutual movements that we realize they have been chained to one another like that for weeks. Among the Spaniards, we now clearly recognize Bermudez, Perucho, and Fuenterrabia; they curse while pushing the Indians who are trying to free a cannon that is stuck in the sand.

Llamas trail with strange cages on their backs which, upon closer inspection, we recognize as chicken coops with hens balanced dizzily inside on their perches, fluffing themselves up, apparently feeling sick from the constant rocking.

To the rear of the procession, Aguirre rides and then stops abruptly at a trio of Spaniards who are busying themselves with a fourth man. He has sore feet and is unable to move on; he tries nevertheless, stubborn and silent.

"Arnalte," says Aguirre to a young Hidalgo, "you take his things, and let him carry his sword." Aguirre digs his spurs into his horse and, riding away, shouts at his men: "Give him a horse, now we need everyone."

Aguirre rides alongside the procession from front to rear; it looks more orderly here on the plain and we can now behold the full extent of their equipment. Only now are we struck by a howling pack of giant hounds running about, gasping and scaring the Indians. Apparently they have been trained for Indians, since every now and then they snarl threateningly and start snapping at the Indians, forcing them to fall out of line. Aguirre stops by his daughter's sedan and slowly rides beside it awhile. Flores seizes her father's hand and kisses it. Neither of them utters a word. Mum, Flores gazes back at a dead Indian who has been left along the way. His bare soles are covered with thick bruised skin. Prolonged ' silence, then Aguirre rides on to the front.

Carvajal wanders on foot with a staff in his hand, the wind blowing his frock forward, making it billow and flap. Aguirre salutes him with a glance. While moving ahead, Carvajal prays with his rosary without moving his lips. He gives the impression of being a tough methodical person.

Descent into the Urubamba Valley

A gloomy valley, densely overgrown with the beginning of the Amazon jungle. The green slopes are dropping steeply downward, following the meanderings of the Urubamba River which rushes way below. How far the slopes are reaching up cannot be discerned because, further above, the valley is closed in by an oscillating veil of vapor and fog. The slopes vanish in the seething steam up into nowhere. Just the muffled roar of the rapids. From the gathering clouds of steam, hummingbirds whir into the deep.

The trek works its way forward. With almost inconceivable difficulty, a heavy cannon is lowered between the trees. The Indians have to fulfill this terrible task. It is so steep, and the slopes are already so densely overgrown, that one can hardly lead the horses down by their bridle. They slip and refuse to be drawn down any further. The two sedans must be borne down empty as Inez and Flores, holding hands, lifting their long skirts, are steadied and supported by Spaniards. Ursua helps Inez and Arnalte, the young Hidalgo reaches out with his hand to Flores from further below. Climbing, Flores almost lends the impression of being a child.

All of a sudden, shouts from above, excitement. Twigs are crackling, a crash is heard and, with a hollow sound close to the women, a weighty cannon crashes down into the deep, cutting a swathe through the undergrowth. A dead pig comes sliding down after it. Far below, the two fall into the rapids of the brown boiling Urubamba.

The chained Indians are in peculiar straits, for if one.of them slips, a whole row goes with him. The highland Indians are already beginning to suffer at this point; nearly all of them have caught colds and some are just staggering on.

We catch sight of a sitting Indian who has been unchained because he is too ill. He is shaking from a fever and draws in his breath with short gasps, like someone with pneumonia. A dog sniffs at him, snarling. They confront each other motionlessly, for a long time, and the dog grinds its teeth at the dying person: a gruesome picture.

Some Spaniards try to drag the llamas onward, but the animals' fright is greater. They have planted their feet into the soft moist soil and only permit themselves to be pulled by the neck. They resist unto death. From deep down, cries are discernible through the rear of the waters, but no one can tell what they mean.

By the Urubamba River

On a very narrow path, where a horse can scarcely support itself, the vanguard has stopped, all of them holding on to something so they won't slip into the raging torrent. They seem to be somewhat helpless, with only Aguirre apparently cool and master of the situation. Gonzalo Pizarro pretends to be calm. "For all of this," he says, "we shall be richer than anyone else before us."

Night camp by the river

Drawn out lengthily along the river, the troops are camping on a stretch of ground which is but one foot in breadth and slopes steeply down. Along the riverbank the flickering fires are drawn out lengthily.

Pizarro, Ursua, Aguirre and the monk are sitting together in deliberation. "When the river widens and is no longer so wild, then we will have made it," Ursua says. "We shall see," says Aguirre. Gonzalo Pizarro presses the point that boats must be built forthwith so some of the equipment can be conveyed by water. The animals and the main troops could then move on more easily along the river. Before too long they would have to stop counting on the Indians because the climate would not agree with them. But they could not have possibly foreseen that.

A Spaniard tends the fire and serves the men a hot drink, trying simultaneously to overhear something. With a barely perceptible hand gesture Pizarro sends him away. Aguirre contradicts Pizarro; very composed, he says it would be unwise, it would be madness in fact, to launch the boats now, the waters would be much too wild, it could not possibly work. Pizarro is rather puzzled, and therefore Ursua comes to his assistance, stating that the leader thus far had judged everything well, it was simply in the nature of his family. "Your Honor," says Ursua, "where there is a Pizarro, there is Honor and gold as well." Aguirre is silent.

Another campfire. Some wild-looking figures crouch around it in a very narrow space. The water is gurgling nearby. The Indians won't hold out much longer, one of them says, as they are so frail that they will perish from something as ridiculous as colds and measles. They're not used to anything and have no power to resist. "Not even flies die from a cold, have you ever heard flies sneeze?" Perucho asks. They all laugh crudely.

A more distant campfire, glowing only faintly. Indians have flocked closely together, we can see just their faces in the obscurity. Dark eyes in the dark. Baltasar, in handcuffs, is with his people and speaks to them very gently in the Quechua Indian dialect. He seems to comfort his people, uttering very soft and subtle words which we do not understand. The Indians cower motionlessly, almost in devout wonder, slowly comprehending their doom. The scene is profoundly serious and sad.

On the riverbank

Several days must have passed, for the Spaniards
have built boats, ten in all, and they are completely laden with equipment. The boats are
somewhat primitive and colorless, they seem
bulky but solid. On each of four boats they have
fastened a cannon, plus sacks with provisions
and casks with powder. Chutes have been
fashioned from wooden planks and lead directly
into the whirling brown water. Everyone is ready
to set out and awaits a sign from Gonzalo
Pizarro. A little further downriver we distinguish
about twenty carelessly-made graves, each of
which bears a cross made of two sticks tied
together. Indians are cowering there. Apparently
these are the graves of Indians, for their number
has diminished considerably. The Indians look
callously up into the seething mist. They turn
their heads like a single man and look up high into the clouds.

"It is time," says Pizarro. The boats are laun-
ched, but then a catastrophe. After only a few
feet, the first boats capsize and sink in the
violent rapids. Utter confusion on shore while the
boats shatter. In the water, Spaniards fight for
their lives, pulled down by their heavy armor,
coming up again for brief intervals. The cannon
sink with the provisions while a powder-filled
cask spins in a whirlpool. A dog jumps into the
water. Seven out of ten boats are shattered; the
remaining three fight against capsizing while being pulled forward furiously. They disappear

beyond the first bend in the river, drifting along, rocking, the crew struggling wordlessly. We realize that, inevitably, one mile further on, they will drown as well.

For a long time the camera takes an interest in the raging waters. Our ears catch the excitement shot through with wild shouts. "God have mercy on our sins!" we hear Carvajal cry.

March along the river

Steep slopes, disappearing above into clouds of steam, the heat has increased. The number of men has lessened considerably, just fifteen Indians have survived, and some of these are recognizably sick at first sight. Baltasar still looks quite strong.

There is only a lone pig left; it keeps sinking into the soft, boggy ground up to its belly.

Then a dead llama in the jungle, over which thousands upon thousands of fire ants fly. Clouds of flies are buzzing about. There are but a few dogs left, but they seem to have grown wild rather quickly, and scarcely stay close to their group any more. With their swords and knives, the Spaniards labor their way through undergrowth and liana labyrinths. They are soaked through with sweat, and thick swarms of mosquitoes are dancing around every single man. Damp foliage everywhere, wet with rain, closing as the men pass in their wake, like water.

21

Then a boggy place where the horses can hardly move on; they refuse to budge. Some Spaniards advance into the smacking morass, dragging the horses behind them by the bridle. At the edge of the bog luggage is piling up. On the opposite side of the bog stands a man with a horse, and both are infested with leeches sucking away at them. The soldier is trying to get rid of the leeches with a little salt. No one is talking, it is a silent frightful fight for every inch.

From the river Urubamba, which is visible now and then through the foliage at their side, a deep roaring sound rises only to be thrown back by the walls, thus sounding like an endless waterfall. This and the wicked whirring of mosquitoes.

There, suddenly, a peculiar scene: two Spaniards are embracing a tree, weeping. One of them, deeply enraptured, kneels down and kisses the trunk. Among all the enormous trees overgrown with lianas, this tree seems rather insignificant. Somewhat surprised, a few Spaniards gather around the two who are so moved that they cannot utter a word.

Pizarro approaches them with Aguirre. "What's the matter here?" asks Pizarro. "Cinammon," sobs one of the two, "this is a cinammon tree." There is silence once more, as if every one were ashamed. "Fetch Baltasar," says Pizarro.

A larger gathering of Spaniards crowds around in a circle. Baltasar is thrust forward and the Spaniards push some Indians after him. Pizarro now delivers a brief public address which, apparently, is meant to encourage his men. From Baltasar, who speaks almost without an accent, we learn that the famous king named El Dorado, who reigns over an immeasurably rich land of gold, is said to live where the cinammon trees grow. After him the land was named El Dorado. The houses are said to be covered with golden tiles and the king is so lofty that only his subjects wear clothes, while he himself is dressed in gold dust every morning. In the evening he steps into a lake and the priests rinse him clean, and every time the gold is lost, but the country has so much that no one cares.

By Pizarro's cross-examination we realize that he already knows the whole story behind the title, and that his men actually know everything also, so this speech is merely intended to strengthen their self-confidence and to encourage them. The Indians are questioned by Baltasar, and their answers come quickly, as if learned by heart.

Indeed, upon setting out the Spaniards seem revived. For once they appear to bear their burdens with a more joyful heart, as if it were but a day's march to El Dorado.

Inez and Flores sit beside each other in their sedans. "If I become Queen," Inez says, "you will be the first lady in my court." Flores smiles a bit self-consciously. "I shall do whatever my father tells me to do," Flores says. The sedans are lifted up and forced through the thicket, swaying. In this jungle the sedan-chairs seem to be a sign of civilized schizophrenia.

Aguirre, leading his horse by the bridle, is beside Ursua. He speaks with him confidentially, and we gradually discover that he will try to conspire with Ursua against Pizarro. He complains about some mistaken decisions Pizarro has made. He, Aguirre, had always maintained that Indian sheep or llamas were useless, and that one could not have the whole load of equipment fall on them. Now all of them, mere superfluities to begin with, were all dead. They could no longer count on the Indians either, as the air didn't agree with them down here, and almost all the pigs had perished in the mountains. They must begin rationing the provisions more carefully, for it was not at all certain that they would reach El Dorado in one week's time. Ursua, feeling reassured, agrees because he had thought and said similar things himself, and because Aguirre confides in him more than in their leader, Pizarro. "We are simply in need of a man like Francisco Pizarro," Aguirre says, "Gonzalo Pizarro isn't even his shadow." He says this in such a way that Ursua must think that he, Ursua himself, has the makings of the leader within him. They drag their horses along. Teeming heat, mosquitoes all over, the everywhere putrid humidity. Pearls of sweat are forming on all faces. The buzzing of the mosquitoes is unbearable, and then the roar of the waters and the shrieks of the parrots. The jungle bares all its sounds. The sun can scarcely pass through to the dim decaying ground. Dogged penetration, step by step.

Large camp

Located where the land is a little flatter and allows for some space, there is a large chaotic work camp active in the jungle. Several big trees have been felled and the thick undergrowth cleared away. Bundles of accouterments are scattered about, some howling dogs are tied to branches, five or six smoking fires are burning at once. The clay soil is dank and sticky. The two sedans stand somewhat apart, and a small screen has been erected to protect them from wayward glances. Some beautifully decorated court dresses made of velvet are hanging on a line with a few lace petticoats. A strained silence reigns over the entire camp. Little movement amongst the men.

From the disorderliness of the camp we can deduce the incipient process of dissolution. Clumps of equipment are lying around carelessly in the mud, filthy cages filled with hens are jammed between branches, shields and weaponry are strewn about, a young Indian in a hammock is dozing towards death, motionless. Only five of the horses are left. They seem to be the one thing attended to with extra care. The horses have been groomed and are covered with blankets. The saddles and bridles, too, are kept sufficiently dry and tidy on the tree limbs.

A hollow crash and crackle and rustle becomes audible now near camp. A huge tree sways very slowly to one side sighing, then faster it falls down lengthwise in a tumult, taking everything with it; a second one follows and directly after it, a third. Now we hear the hacking of axes and the sound of saws. One tree falls after another. The camera shows a great fascination for the falling trees.

Great gathering in the camp

The Spaniards are sitting in a circle fully armored, some chained Indians behind them and, set off a bit to the side, the two sedans. Inez and Flores, however, have removed themselves and are listening from a distance. In the center of the circle stands Pizarro who is giving a speech to his men. He tells them they can't go on like this, the provisions are nearly exhausted and everything was getting scarce. One could not yet talk of starvation but some of the men had been doing so the past few days. The terrain was so treacherous that they could hardly proceed, and it was not to be expected that they would reach a populated region in the near future. Therefore, he and his camp foreman Pedro de Ursua and his lieutenant, Lope de Aguirre had made the following decision which had already been drafted by the scrivener into a legal document. They had resolved to build a raft, to man it with men led by Ursua, in order to explore the territory ahead of them and to search for means of subsistence. According to reports from the Indians, they were now approaching some hostile Indian tribes as well, which would endanger the situation. The crew on the raft would have the task of returning within two weeks at most to the main camp here, either by land or by water, and if they hadn't returned by then, it would be concluded that all of them had lost their lives. In such a case, which they hoped wouldn't happen, the remaining expedition here would try to turn back to find refuge in regions where Christians lived. They would place a great deal of hope in the fate of the exploring vanguard, and, naturally, they were hoping to obtain precise data pertaining to the status of the gold country. Baltasar, who was indispensable as an interpreter, was sent with them for that reason. Maybe they would even find traces of the expedition under the valiant captain Orellana who had vanished three years earlier. He did not intend to flatter anyone, and none who were omitted from the party should feel neglected, but he did mean to stress that he had chosen the best of the available men; they were the flower of the Spanish crown and the strong arm of civilized Christianity. God had also given them the most reverend Fray Gaspar de Carvajal for guidance so that he might bring light into the night and darkness of Creation here, and preach the true creed.

They had come to the agreement that the two women would travel with the vanguard, although he did not want the responsibility as it was clearly stated in the document, wishing instead to save it for a different decision; but they would try to make their living situation as pleasant as circumstances would allow, nevertheless. Inez had declared that she had sold all her belongings in order to follow Pedro de Ursua, and that she would rather give up her life voluntarily than not to be by his side; and she had proclaimed this with such grace and self-assurance that one could not help but let her go with them. As for Flores, Aguirre had prevailed in his wish to keep her under the protection of her father's arm since she was still in the first flower of her youth.

All of this had been decided, and as a symbol of their agreement they now would sign the document which had been formulated today, three days before the New Year. Thus they would be able to present it to the Indian Council upon their return.

Pizarro is given the document and sets it on a small improvised table, where pen and ink are already lying at his disposal. Pizarro withdraws a small metal plate from his pocket on which his signature has been carved. We watch how Pizarro copies his name with the pen in a clumsy hand. Then Ursua, Aguirre and some of the officers sign, and at last, the Dominican monk.

Departure of the raft

There lies the river in the first morning mist, a solid raft afloat upon it with the two sedans standing in the middle, and a roof of bark fastened to four poles. The heavy tree trunks are held

together by metal hooks, all else being faste...
with cords and ropes. Coarse tow-ropes hold the
raft to the bank of the fast flowing river, and in
spite of its weight, it rolls slightly with the pressure of the waters. The raft is loaded to the brim
with equipment: armor, weapons, barrels, a cannon, and even a horse, standing to the side.
Then, cages with hens, provisions, sacks with
corn and seed, fuel, rope, arquebuses, and some
pans.

The Spaniards are trying to get a second horse
aboard over some wooden planks, but despite
having shielded its eyes, the horse resists with all
its might, rearing up so high that the men consider it too dangerous. "Let it be," says Aguirre,
"it has its reasons." "One horse will certainly be
enough to frighten the Indians," says Ursua.

Already the raft is fully manned, there is barely
enough room for forty men. They are all cramm-
ed close to each other. At both the front and rear
of the raft stands a man with a clumsy oar which
serves to maneuver the raft. The cars are lashed
with rope to a fork of smooth wood.

At dawn, Carvajal, the Dominican monk, is on
board reading the Mass. He gives Holy Commu-
nion to those on board first, and then to the
kneeling Spaniards at the riverbank who are left
behind. Deeply devoted and enraptured, the last
surviving Indians are taking it on land.

The main rope is hacked through with a sword; it
is a laconic, nearly speechless farewell. Baltasar
has come to the edge of the raft and kneels
before the last of his people, his bound hands
folded. The Indians are clapping their hands on

anguish and despair. Now, with a
... frees itself and begins drifting very
... ow it goes up," cries Pizarro. "Now
...own," says Aguirre. There is steam and
...ng mist over the tropical slopes, and the
proceeds.

On the river

The raft is drifting rapidly now, pushed forward
from bend to bend unimpeded, turning round in
circles repeatedly, the landscape slips by speedily.
The raft moans and groans, and the waters of
the river Urubamba are rushing sluggishly. The
jungle slopes continue to rise up infinitely,
although not as steeply as at first. Clouds are
gathering over the canyon. The oarsmen work
hard and incessantly, but in these wild waters
they can barely manage to keep the raft in the
middle of the river. Sometimes it drifts close to
the shore where twigs and lianas and exposed
roots dangle over the water, and the men on
board must lower their heads and steady
themselves in order to avoid being pulled overboard. There are some rapids which turn the raft
with a jerk on its axis, intimidating the men
somewhat, including Ursua who wants to prove
himself leader. "For every hour," says Aguirre,
"we would need a day on land."

The raft drifts onward and, upon hitting a sand-bar with a jolt, some bundles of accouterments are lost. Hands stretch forth vainly to catch some of it again. Only Perucho lifts a bag filled with provisions on board, using a fork for propping up arquebuses. Some tree trunks have dislodged themselves dangerously and rub against each other with a groaning sound. Water is slapping the trunks. The men have to be careful not to trap their feet between the trunks. Creaking, the raft again hits sandy ground.

Inez and Flores have sat down anxiously in their two sedans which are standing close together. Inez is holding Flores' hands in hers, both await their fates patiently. Ursua approaches the pair to lend encouragement. Once they had escaped the worst torrents, they would be safe. And, as things appeared, there were no more torrents expected further down. The Indians had asserted this unanimously. The men gaze ahead eagerly, anticipating something around every bend. "Beyond this bend will be a house, perhaps," says Fuenterrabia. And while everyone maintains an incredulous silence, he adds that this could easily be the case.

All at once there is confusion and chaos on one side of the raft, because the horse has taken fright and is rearing up. In its excitement, it steps halfway onto a barrel which makes it rear up even more. It jerks its head hard as foam gathers around its mouth and flanks. Some of the men try to save themselves from the mad trampling hooves by moving to the narrowest space thereby adding to the general confusion. The horse is on the verge of leaping overboard, simply refusing to calm down. Two men succeed at last in getting hold of the bridles and pushing the horse backwards onto a less-congested spot. Its forelegs get caught in some of the ropes, which are cautiously untied by Arnalte who courageously attends. Arnalte succeeds in becalming the horse completely. Baltasar is sitting all this time close by the dangerously trampling hooves, petrified with fright, and in his terror, unable to move whatsoever.

Flores has noticed Baltasar's paralysis and takes a few steps towards him from her sedan. She attempts to draw him aside a little, but the terror of the Indian is still too deeply rooted. Some of the Spaniards laugh at him cruelly, saying the Indian is more afraid than a girl, that he is shitting in his pants. Flores suddenly starts to cry. "Baltasar," she says, "it's a good horse, it's only frightened." Baltasar looks at her in strange wonderment. "But it's a stallion, and they call it Clodoaldo," says Flores.

Sandbank in the river

It is a blazing-hot noon, and at a point where the river has broadened a bit the raft has hit a sandbank. The current is still very strong. Some distance away, a few alligators are lying on the white sand of the sandbank in motionless avidity.

Several Spaniards have stepped into the water and are trying to free the raft with poles. Others poke at the water with their poles to chase away the alligators that might come close. A blue-black thunderstorm is brewing on the horizon, the pitch-black clouds towering heaven high, lit up already by flashes of lightning. The thunder is not yet audible. Excited screaming of birds in the jungle. "Heave-ho," cry the men on board, and when the raft half-frees itself they cry, "Come on!" "Come on, come on," cries the parrot, which Perucho has taken aboard with him. The bird flaps its wings and ruffles its feathers. The horse is standing there, frightened by the violent movements of the poles, nervously tramping on its narrow space.

Chimalpahin, whom they call Baltasar, is sitting a short distance away, and with faraway eyes he gazes at the clouds. All has become deathly still, but no one notices because of their work. Only Chimalpahin is looking about right now. The birds in the forest have become mute, no wind is blowing, and yet the flashes of lightning are already visible. Quite casually we catch sight of an arrow sticking in the wood as if it belonged there. Then suddenly, an outcry. Screaming, a soldier stands up with a start, an arrow stuck in his calf. And at the same time, the alligators disappear into the water with a hollow splash.

Shouts break out, wild movement. "To arms!" shouts Aguirre above all else. He roars at some soldiers, who have lost their heads and jump about helplessly, to go ahead and fire. Ursua and Arnalte, together with some Spaniards, have armed themselves with shields and thrown themselves in front of the two sedans. Wild excitement and, what nobody notices, no more arrows. The sultry forest lies motionless as the first shots thunder from the arquebuses which are supported by the gunner on iron forks. "What are you aiming at?" someone shrieks. "Fire, you ass!" bellows Ursua wildly. Then, as if by themselves, the thunderous shots cease and the men become sober once again. One of them declares aloud that since there were no more arrows, the enemy was probably very few in number. Ursua asks whether anybody had seen one. No one can remember.

The wounded man is seated between two bundles, cursing; they have already extracted the arrow from his blood-gushing leg. The arrow wanders from hand to hand while the wounded man is seeing if he can still move his toes properly. Ursua orders them to continue firing into the forest for the sake of security and to chase away the enemy. The mouths of the cannon roar and smoke and in between, deep silence. The thunderstorm overhead refuses to draw close; in the distance its mute flashes are still flickering.

In the feverish swelter, with shots still being fired, the men succeed with a strenuous effort in freeing the raft. As the raft drifts on, there is just enough time for the men to be pulled onto the tree trunks. But some of the trunks have nearly come apart and some of the ropes are almost totally frayed. Several men on board are trying to re-attach two trunks with iron clamps, all this makeshift at most. The current is no longer so strong however, and the steep slopes of the canyon now widen a bit. Dense swarms of malignant mosquitoes are swarming around the men on board. The jungle has regained its voice. Voices of birds and monkeys squabbling in some tree tops, thousands of other sounds. The men suffer in the broiling heat.

The towering clouds are now approaching, almost continual flashes of lightning and the distant grumble of thunder. Rain suddenly floods down, hot and heavy, hardly ever in single drops, almost entirely in a solid mass. Everyone is instantly drenched and they hardly attempt to cover their heads with their shields. All is soaked, the dresses, the bundles, the provisions; we behold a Spaniard, whose armored sleeve serves as a drainpipe. Thunder and lightning are very near now, the horse shies with fright and the jungle is one dull roar. The water in the river seems to boil, steam issuing forth from the surface. All on board are cowering, motionless, while lightning flashes incessantly. Heavy crashes of thunder echo out from the steep slopes.

Inside the sedan, soaked through as well, Inez is sitting, praying mutely with a rosary. Aguirre is beside his daughter's sedan, holding a shield in front of the curtain so that not too much rain may penetrate within.

Campsite on a sandy spot

The raft has been tied to the shore in a flat sandy place, objects lie scattered about in the sultry sun to dry. Steam is rising everywhere. Several fully-armored Spaniards have positioned themselves against possible aggressors by facing towards the jungle, some take a few cautious steps into the steaming wilderness. The trees are still dripping profusely. The horse is on shore eating leaves. Some Spaniards are digging in the sand for turtle eggs. The curtains in the sedans are pulled up to dry; Juan de Arnalte politely spreads a mat on the sand for the women, then he withdraws again. Lively activity everywhere. Perucho is alone on board with his parrot, trying to teach him the term "El Dorado".

The Spaniards have constructed two charcoal kilns on the sand, using thin tree trunks and strong branches. Both pyres are smoking away, with the men paying close attention so it doesn't start smoking too heavily. If too much smoke develops, they deaden it by covering it with sand. Ursua, Aguirre and Guzman are walking through the camp, carefully inspecting every object. They pick up some pans and a short chain, then they collect the iron forks from the arquebuses. "You have to make yourself wooden forks," says Aguirre to one of the men. Gradually we realize that they are searching for iron. They even remove the horse's shoes. The ground is soft here, anyway, Ursua reflects. Even the iron work on the handles of the sedans is taken off. A brief discussion arises around Baltasar, as to whether or not they should remove his handcuffs. Ultimately Ursua is against it, because he fears that Baltasar might flee into the jungle. Proud Baltasar sits entranced, not listening to what they are saying.

Camp, early morning

The raft is completely cleared now, all the luggage being scattered about in the sand. The piles of charcoal are gone, and in one spot the Spaniards have built an improvised forge. A stone serves as an anvil, and from a coarse piece of leather the men have made a simple bellows, on which two men alternate working. The Spaniards are busy forging iron clamps and nails. It is very tiresome work.

There is a peculiarly tense atmosphere in the camp, no one dares to talk out loud. Furtive glances are cast aside, at a distance, Ursua and Aguirre are quarreling, barely able to restrain themselves. The men eye one another wordlessly while working. Something is in the air.

Ursua calls the men together, most of whom already sense what is happening, and he declares, reminding them of his authority as Major General, that he has decided to return. It probably would take two weeks to get back to the main camp by land; they had seen from the raft how difficult the terrain really was, and by land the danger posed by the hostile natives would increase.

Aguirre, his most intimate friends gathered around him, curtly explains to Ursua that he will not follow this order, for their task was to explore the territory and supply themselves with food, and so far they hadn't achieved either of the two since nothing of importance had been encountered yet. In two days the powerful current had moved them so far away from the starting point that, under these circumstances, a return seemed senseless, as they would have exhausted all their provisions by the time they reached the camp and, furthermore, they would put an additional burden on Pizarro's shoulders by consuming his food. Things have progressed to such an extent that there was nothing to do but advance; and why had he, Ursua, given orders to forge nails if he didn't intend to mend the raft completely. That is not the only ambiguity he has shown. Aguirre calls upon the men, in the glorious name of the Spanish Crown, to continue their expedition at their own risk. He recalls Hernando Cortez in Mexico who, once he had sailed, had also received orders to return, but Cortez defied the order, and today he has riches and glory. Now it lay in their own power to alter the course of history, now it awaited their mighty grip.

The men are moved, and despite Ursua's order to be quiet, Aguirre continues talking to the men in strong inflammatory words. Most of them are indecisive, and only Aguirre's closest friends, Bermudez, Guzman, and Fuenterrabia, give the impression of unity. But Aguirre knows that secretly he speaks from the heart of the majority.

Ursua is utterly enraged, and makes the mistake of ordering two men to seize the rebel Aguirre and put him in chains. The two timidly lay their hands on Aguirre. At this moment, happening so quickly that one hardly realizes how it came about, Fuenterrabia's musket explodes with a thunderous burst and, hit from the shortest of distances, Ursua falls flat on this face in the sand, mortally wounded. A wild commotion breaks out, Inez comes flying to the scene, Aguirre's men grab their arms. The horse gallops to and fro, trampling the sand. "Stop! No fighting!" thunders Aguirre at the mindless ones. He succeeds in subduing the initial panic, no one really knows whom to fight. Inez kneels beside Ursua who has turned to stone, and Carvajal the monk has pressed a small crucific into his hands and listens with his ear close to the mouth of the dying man who is trying to say something. But Ursua is unable to utter a word, and rapidly his last ounce of life dies away. Flores runs about, completely upset, trying in vain to find bandages. An officer rises up against Aguirre and commands several men to kill Fuenterrabia and Aguirre on the spot. The men hesitate, looking for support. "Execute him," says Aguirre with an icy voice. He makes a hardly-discernible movement of the head. Bermudez, Perucho, and Fuenterrabia kneel down and aim at the officer, who first steps back a bit, but then, courageously, advances toward Aguirre, sword in hand and resolved to do anything. Almost simultaneously, shots are heard. The officer is thrown back a ways, he is dead on the spot. The white sand surrounding him soaks up the blood. "Anyone else?" asks Aguirre.

Camp, towards evening

Evening's mood has spread over the sandy place. Mosquitoes are dancing in the last rays of sunlight, a few big butterflies are staggering by, drunk with the jungle. At the edge of the jungle, but still in the sand, two graves have been dug side by side, adorned with wooden crosses. Paralyzed with pain, almost without willpower, Inez kneels before Ursua's grave. She is kneeling as if she has not yet awakened from her bewilderment.

All of the Spaniards have gathered at the raft. The objects are still strewn about the landing place, and the raft is completely empty. The men are discussing whom they should take as their leader, and Aguirre, who leads the discussion, realizes that the others fear his boundless ambition and untamed energy and knows that his time has not yet come. All of the men have taken the precaution of appearing with arms, as the situation is not unequivocal yet, and everyone distrusts everyone else .

As a matter of course, Aguirre proposes that Fernando de Guzman be elected Major General. Guzman is of lofty descent and one of the most experienced fighters ever to have fought for the Spanish crown in Peru. Aguirre distinctly believes therefore that no party will form against him. Guzman is extremely frightened and tries to keep the burden at bay, but Aguirre continues steadfastly to single out Guzman's merits, recalling the conquering of the fortress Sascahuyaman. Guzman must accept this high honor, but as he still resists, the Spaniards try persuading him from all sides to accept their wishes. They would willingly serve then under his able guidance, and further, they would appoint Lope de Aguirre as his deputy, since he had cooly analyzed the situation and expressed all of their innermost wishes. Only in this way would they all achieve riches and honor. Who is for Guzman, asks Aguirre. All raise their hands and, over the head of Guzman, they appoint him Major General. Who is for Aguirre as his deputy, asks Perucho. This time, too, all raise their hands; tributes resound and the council begins to dissolve.

At a distance, on the edge of the sandbank, Inez is visible, kneeling, her face as white as the sand; she is confessing to Carvajal, the monk who stands beside her. Carvajal is wearing his shawl, and has put one end of it on Inez' shoulder. He listens patiently while she apparently tries to get her life clear, she looks waxen and calm. They remain there for a long time, motionless, the two of them. The sun has already disappeared behind the mountain slope. Carvajal gives her his blessing and Inez rises, fully composed, as if she has summed up her life. From the jungle, sounds of a million beings are audible.

Several fires are burning and along the edge of
the jungle, armed guards are watching. They
have positioned themselves in pairs. Around the
fires, the evening meal is almost over. Some of
the Spaniards are baking a few milky translucent
turtle eggs, which are covered with a soft skin, in
the faint, glimmering ashes. Subdued conversation, the men lying leisurely and expectantly, trying to protect themselves from the mosquitoes.
Aguirre walks calmly between the fires, talking
quietly to individual groups of Spaniards. Bermudez, Perucho, and Fuenterrabia are whispering to each other. It looks as if something has
been planned for the coming day.

Juan de Arnalte is sitting by the sedan with
Flores, whispering to her of his mountains at
home and of his brothers and the waterfall
behind his house. He seems to be homesick, and
Flores is aware of this, listening to him patiently
and with great interest. Aguirre disturbs the two.
He sends Arnalte away, he should go and sleep,
for at midnight he will have to watch. This New
Year's Day was the beginning of significant
events, this will be a meaningful year, all of them
will alter the course of history.

When Aguirre is alone with Flores, he tells her to
inform Inez that he, Aguirre, will not do her any
harm, on the contrary, he would treat her as a
lady of honor. She was compelled only by the
course of events to follow the expedition further,
even if this did not agree with her wishes. We

notice that Aguirre has inhibitions which keep him from talking to Inez personally.

Camp, early morning

Everyone is already up and stirring. While the last iron clamps are fastened to the trunks of the raft, the Spaniards start reloading the raft. At the same time, some men are making a square in the sand with some poles and commence construction of a small wooden dais. Aguirre gives the orders here, whereas Guzman, who is suffering somewhat from diarrhea, supervises the work at the raft. Guzman disappears into the sultry damp jungle and returns with a not-too-happy face, trying, however, to keep his dignity. Aguirre speaks of an important council which must be held before they leave. Guzman is flattered, for he knows the council is for his benefit. The Spaniards are standing in the square now, leaving a free space in the center. Aguirre delivers a gripping speech to his men using very strong words. The time had come to take common fate into their own hands, only the brave are helped by fate, it casts off the cowardly. It was necessary to legalize all further undertakings, and so he and Guzman had mutually decided to appoint Diego de Bermudez scrivener. It was necessary now to decide for themselves, or else

43

once they had conquered El Dorado, they would have to relinquish the fruits of their efforts to the undeserving. It was therefore necessary to free themselves from the bonds of the Spanish crown, and to proclaim their leader Emperor of Peru and Dorado. Would they agree to that. "Yes," cry the enchanted men. A tumult erupts, exultation. Aguirre has directed this farce almost in the style of an operetta.

Aguirre pushes Bermudez and Guzman forward. He declares that overnight he had already formulated a document with Bermudez which he now wants to read to them, in order to ask them for their approval or disapproval. "Caesarean King," reads Aguirre, "by the grace of God, through our Holy Mother, the Holy Roman Church, named King Philipp the Second of Castille, we, the undersigned, have, until yesterday, the first day of the year 1561, after the birth of our savior Jesus Christ, regarded ourselves as your servants and subjects, after we have moved away from your servant Gonzalo Pizarro more than two hundred leagues within two days. Fate, the help of God, and the labor of our own hands have driven us down a river, called by the natives Urubamba, in search of a new land of gold, and we have decided to put an end to the quirks of our Fate. We are the Course of History, and no fruit of this earth shall henceforth be shared. We rebel unto death. We solemnly declare — and our hands shall be torn off and our tongues shall dry up if this is not so — the House of Hapsburg to be devoid of all its rights, and you, Philipp II, King of Castile, dethroned. By dint of this declaration thou art annihilated. In your stead, we proclaim the noble knight from the city of Seville, Fernando de Guzman, Emperor of Peru and Dorado. Flee, flee from here hence, O King, and may God protect your soul."

The Spaniards rejoice, and after the incense has been lit, Carvajal intones the Te Deum. The men wave their weapons overhead as Aguirre leads Guzman to a shabby improvised throne in the center of the square. A seat on the podium has been upholstered with one of Flores' velvet gowns. Guzman feels exceedingly honored, though half resisting still, and has objections to the kind of throne it is. "What is a throne?" growls Aguirre in his ear, pushing him forward, "A piece of wood, covered with a piece of velvet."

Guzman takes his seat and Aguirre, the first to kneel down, seizes his hand and kisses it. The other men follow his example, one pushing behind the other. Then everyone signs the document except the two women and Baltasar who have no right to do so. The men fire their muskets and start hailing Guzman who accepts this homage gravely, although obviously suffering from a belly ache.

Now they all form a great operatic tableau, and with ritualistic gestures, Guzman is led by Carvajal and Aguirre from his throne to the earth. Guzman boards the raft with solemn steps and, among the universal rejoicing of his people, gives the signal for departure.

On the river, mouth of the Ucayali

The river has broadened a bit, flowing more
slowly, the mountain slopes recede undramatical-
ly. The raft is drifting calmly, but without delay.
On the riverside, whole trees and overhanging
limbs are dragging in the water. On the right-
hand side a wide hidden valley opens up, and
coming closer, we behold the mouth of a big
river carrying yellowish-brown water, and upon
which drifts a striking number of fallen branches,
even whole trees, their roots outstretched toward
the steaming sky. And there, fully bloated, a
dead tapir as big as a mule floats past the Spaniards' raft. The river to the right is apparently
larger. For miles, the darker waters of the Urubamba are not mingling with the waters of the
Ucayali which carries large quantities of clay. In
the middle of the already-gaping river runs a
clear and colorful line of demarcation.

The Spaniards are very curious, and they beckon
information from Baltasar who, however, is un-
sure about this. No information had reached
the Incas from such a faraway realm, but he did
know of a big river to the south called "Ucayali". Following Aguirre's instructions assiduous-
ly, Diego Bermudez is employed in making a
rough sketch as quickly as possible before the
raft has drifted past completely.

The men suffer under the oppressive sweltering
heat, sweating without being cooled. The raucous
quarreling of the monkeys carries from the jungle
across the waters, growing to such an extent that

the parrots join in, as if they were asking for
silence. We can distinguish some movement in
the tree tops, and in the dense foliage, the
squeaking proceeds from tree to tree.

Since passing the mouth, the horse has become
restless, although there is no obvious reason for
this. The stallion jerks his head and shies from
something we do not see. The Spaniards aboard
are listening, but they cannot discern a thing in
the motionless jungle. The trees mysteriously
mask their own trance. The horse nervously
stamps at the ground, its dance creating disorder
in the ordered assembly surrounding it. One
Spaniard, shoving hastily, pushes another one
and his helmet gets lost overboard. Hands are
stretching out for it, but the helmet has swiftly
sunk.

The horse is jumping now, and gets bundles of
equipment between its hooves, which makes it
shy away even more. A man has taken hold of
the bridle and yanks it down, but the stallion
fights back with all its might. One half of the
raft is in an uproar. Chimalpahin is particularly
perturbed, and Inez, praying with her rosary in
the open sedan, briefly glances up from her
trance. It takes a long time for the horse to calm
down, and just when it seems to be tranquil once
more, it jumps forward with a mighty leap right
into a group of Spaniards who are preparing a
meal over a small fire they have lighted between
some stones. Sparks fly about and chaos breaks
out. "The powder!" someone cries out, horrified, and now we catch sight of a powder barrel,
where some spilled gunpowder is swiftly igniting

in the direction of the bunghole.

Panic-stricken, everyone flees to the edge of the raft, two men fall down and jump overboard. Aguirre advances coolly, and almost provocatively, he slowly lifts the barrel up and throws it into the water. There it glimmers on, drifting forward somewhat faster than the raft. Everyone on the raft has thrown himself to the floor, with Aguirre alone standing, serenely assessing the scene. Chimalpahin is sitting, unconcerned. A dull heavy detonation follows with a pillar of water shooting up in the air and splattering over the raft. Then, massive waves, the vessel rocks and sways, and a deep silence settles over the water and over the jungle. All voices have hushed. The two Spaniards who had fallen overboard and were clutching the edge of the raft are pulled up onto the dryness by helping hands. The horse seems restful now, but the excitement of the men lasts a long time. Slowly, order returns. A long, long view over the passing jungle. The forest is steaming dreamily, not one leaf rustles. Butterflies are dancing in the open air. Damp impenetrable labyrinths of leaves, exposed roots and trees, strangled to death by lianas. A cloud of whirring hummingbirds rises high, hovering motionless above the tree-tops. A hundred thousand strange sounds. The water flows lazily, caked with clay. Only very far away, in the background, mountain slopes overgrown with jungle are visible. Clouds are piling up everywhere, as they do before a thunderstorm.

Lunch on board

Food is distributed on board, but we realize at first glance that the food is being severly rationed. Not one of the men murmurs, we even notice one storing away a small supply of fruit for worse occasions. The Spaniards draw water from the brown river and drink it in a manner that suggests they quit caring quite some time ago. The horse is feeding on a heap of twigs and leaves amassed in front of it. Its forelegs are fettered. Aguirre, eating delibertately, sits among the men. Before starting on his own ration, Juan de Arnalte has politely served the ladies who apparently have been given a little more. The women have made themselves comfortable in their sedans.

While they are eating, the eyes of the men keep wandering secretly to the middle of the raft where, under the cover of a little bark roof, Guzman feasts as always. A table made from a little box and covered with a clean cloth is placed before him, and Guzman is the only one to receive proper cutlery. He has appointed a man cupbearer, who stands behind him and is not yet allowed to eat. Such a large quantity of food has been piled up in front of Guzman that one knows he cannot eat it all by himself. The men on board are silent, full of animosity, the happily feasting Guzman is unaware of this. With a graceful gesture he lifts the mug, and the man behind him pours brownish river water into it. Guzman obviously relishes his new role.

Flores has left her sedan and carries part of her food to Baltasar, who has been given hardly anything, and who has only begun to eat slowly with his fettered hands after a long interval of introspection. Flores climbs over some luggage until she reaches him. She sets a bowl before him. Baltasar slowly glances up, awakening from his trance. Flores climbs back to her sedan without anyone taking offense. A strange silence reigns over the raft when, suddenly, the jungle petrifies. All sounds have died as if by some blow, with deathly threatening stillness spreading.

A few men grow wary and listen, Aguirre glances about as only Guzman continues feasting joyfully. A man drawing a bowlful of water bends backwards. The man beside him slumps back with a weird expression, his morsel of food getting caught in his throat while he sinks into the river, legs upturned. At the same time the water commences to boil and seethe, as if the man were made of red-hot iron. There is a furious battle in the water, and now we recognize the piranhas, an enormous swarm of ravenous rapacious fish.

The man with the bowl tries to grab hold of the sinking man but misses him, and the piranhas snatch him with teeth like razor blades. The oarsman to the rear succeeds in pulling up with a pole the man's armor which had been drifting in the seething water. A hand sticks out of the water and two Spaniards grope for it hastily, momentarily withdrawing a boney arm that was eaten until nothing but skeleton remained. Only the hand is still where the hand should be. They are paralyzed with horror on board. The hand wears a ring and bears a scar on the outside. The boiling spot in the water is left behind, the raft drifts on.

A view of the jungle, nothing perceptible, nothing stirs, still no sound.

On board the men have jumped up amid a confusion of highly excited voices. Inez and Flores turn aside, shuddering. One man alone sits motionless by his bowl, a pensive expression on his face, his fork sticking on his food. He is leaning against a cluster of luggage. Perucho's parrot has heeded the excitement. He screams "El Dorado." In his agitation, Fuenterrabia nudges the sitting man with his foot, and his fork falls to the floor with a clatter. Fuenterrabia is startled and turns around. "What?" says Fuenterrabia, attracting the attention of the other men. "He's done in," one of them says. The Spaniards push the sitting man a little, ever so gently, but the man is dead indeed and bends forward incredibly slowly. Now we notice a dart sticking in the nape of his neck, it is barely as big as a knitting needle and feathered behind with a ball of twisted cotton. Carvajal, the Dominican monk, is the first to regain his composure and extracts the dart from the neck of the dead man, carefully laying the corpse on the floor of the raft.

The dart, in closeup. It wanders from hand to hand, inspiring awe. The tip has been sharpened like a needle and thickened with a piece of bast cord. A sticky milky liquid coats it. "Poison," says Fuenterrabia, and "Poison," says Bermudez. "To arms!" shouts Aguirre. "Fire your muskets!"

Confusion arises once again as the Spaniards fire about wildly with their muskets, throwing themselves down behind their shields for protection. Here, all at once, the jungle seems to regain its voice, birdcalls are heard starting up again. "Come on, come on," Perucho's parrot croaks. The rolling gunshots are dying, and clouds of bluish smoke drift over the raft.

How could this have been possible, Aguirre asks his men, who have calmed down a bit. Yes, how could this have been possible, Guzman repeats, his napkin still stuck in his collar. Judging from the size of the arrow, reflects Perucho, it must have been a midget bow about nine inches long. He could not understand, however, how one could shoot so far with a bow as small as that, extending his hand to show. They had been at least a quarter of a league away from the riverside. But Fuenterrabia objects, saying that the arrow had no notch in back for a string, and besides, it was much too thin. Everyone tries to solve the riddle, Chimalpahin is unable to provide any information either. They are still oppressed by the alluring calmness of the jungle, and try to deaden their fright by way of their intense involvement with the blow-dart.

Dusk over the river

The raft drifts downriver. With a slow beating of oars on both sides, the men are keeping the raft in the middle of the river. We see the raft from a distance of about three hundred feet. Incense is rising, and all of the Spaniards have gathered on one end of the raft, kneeling. Carvajal prays as we hear their singing drift over the river. Two men now lift the corpse, which is sewn inside a linen shroud, and let it slide slowly overboard. The monk makes the gesture of a blessing. The raft drifts onward, calmly, and disappears. On both sides of the river, the jungle is already very dark.

Day on the river, sultry day

Aguirre stands at the front of the raft, gazing ahead expectantly towards a great bend in the river. It is an oppresively hot day and Aguirre's clothes are sticky with sweat. The men around him look noticeably more depraved, the clothes of one of them starting to rot. The men take hardly any measures to protect themselves from the mosquitoes which besiege them relentlessly. All have obviously lost weight. We catch sight of a Spaniard, nibbling meticulously at the stalk of a manioc root without caring about the dirt.

At the rear end of the raft, the men have constructed a little outhouse on a boom above the river which consists of four poles with canvas stretched between them. There, Guzman loiters about, apparently suffering severely from diarrhea. He keeps the place occupied most of the time, still trying, however, to look awe-inspiring.

In their sedans standing side by side, the two women are suffering gravely from the damp heat. Flores fans herself feebly with a delicate laced fan, unable to cool herself. Beside her Inez sits peacefully in a beautiful velvet dress, praying with her rosary. She does not seem to notice anything around her any more.

Little is said on board, all of them are craning their necks in order to detect something beyond the next bend in the river. Slowly we see that around the bend, the river alone is stretching out further, and to the left and to the right, there is nothing but dense jungle. Bermudez, standing near Aguirre, appropriates the document with which they solemnly take possession of the land to the left and right. Guzman is summoned to sign the document, and then Aguirre also puts his name underneath it with a flourish. He writes Lope de Aguirre; he intends to add something else which, however, he ultimately omits. At certain spots the river is now about four miles wide, then it narrows a bit again before flowing onward ever so lazily. Islands appear more frequently, some are so long that one cannot guess how far drawn out they are. For this reason the river often forks out in several branches. Sandbanks rise up clearly out of the brownish water, as clouds like cotton balls drift overhead.

Inez and Flores are seated next to Baltasar, who is speaking calmly, now and then pushing his hair from his face with both hands which are still bound together with handcuffs. Baltasar talks about the downfall of his people and of his childhood, speaking very softly. They had experienced bolts of lightning and plagues and earthquakes, but what has happened to them now is much greater. His name was Chimalpahin, and his surname was Quauhtlehuanitzin, meaning "the one who speaks". Only his closest relatives, plus the Inca and his family, had the right to look at him, all others were forced to look at the floor before him. "That is the way Nobility declines," says Bermudez bitingly, having listened to them from nearby. Baltasar slowly glances up, keeping silent. "So speak, go on," growls Fuenterrabia, "and don't shit in your pants."

Perucho wants to know how big the golden daggers of El Dorado are, whether they are bigger than the ones from Peru: this big, or this—he spreads his hands and indicates two imaginary sizes, and since he knows that Baltasar cannot spread his hands, he starts howling with laughter at his own joke. More men laugh as Baltasar maintains silence, quite abstracted. "Quiet," says Aguirre, "we still need him." Flores sits weeping to herself. Fuenterrabia tells her that she shouldn't blubber, it was only an Indian, after all.

We take a close look at two Spaniards. They are both sitting right at the edge of the raft, and neither seems to want to fully expose himself to the Indians' poisonous darts out here on the brink. Therefore both struggle slowly, silently, to take the better place away from the other, since it apparently promises superior shelter. They observe each other malevolently, and every time one of them gets a little inattentive, the other nudges him over a bit. Such jostling seems to have ensued for days, for the hostility of the two is gnawing.

Late afternoon

Part of the crew is sitting drowsily on board, the others are stretching their necks, straining to see what is coming around the next bend. Heavy lukewarm rain is falling steadily. The men are talking about El Dorado and how it could best be conquered. If the capital had walls that would be bad, of course, for they had no heavy equipment and a siege would require many more men. "El Dorado, El Dorado," Perucho repeats to his parrot continually, but it croaks and says: "Come on." Perucho has now provided a perch for his bird, upon which it plays about. Yes, says Perucho proudly, a parrot lives to be ninety at least. His was surely eighty already, and it only had a bald ass.

We can clearly determine that rust has formed on the men's armor and that, due to the humidity, the clothes of many have started to rot. Most of them have sore spots around their necks from the rubbing of the armor and the continuous flow of salty sweat. A few seem to be suffering from fever, and they always feel cold in spite of all the heat. Guzman has apparently gotten the fever on top of his diarrhea, for he is always wrapped in a blanket.

Aguirre is sitting with Bermudez working on a map, and he adds some legal notes along the bottom. Bermudez wants to submit it to Guzman for his signature, but Aguirre merely says, "The Emperor has diarrhea." The two men eye one another knowingly. There were but a few bags of corn left and very little food besides, Bermudez allows. They must reach the country of El Dorado soon, or else someone would have to think of something else. Aguirre had noticed that Guzman had secretly held him, Aguirre, responsible for the difficulties with the provisions. The salt was used up completely, and some men had already complained of muscle ache because of this. Aguirre stands there, musing. The rain has abated and is only drizzling slightly.

Perucho sits with his parrot in a circle of Spaniards building castles in the air, how well one would live, and how many servants one would have. They would henceforth build all their cannons of gold, and fire golden balls. The men start naming the provinces and distributing them, and they discuss the offices that they would then hold. Perucho already imagines himself governor. He speaks of conquest and siege, and his motto is: "Billowing sails, holy oaths and ready arms." The men are gradually talking themselves into a state of agitation. Fuenterrabia, busy with his

57

hens, interrupts them, calling over to say that they would finally show the Indians what a rake is.

Carvajal interjects and scolds the men for forgetting that there were other things to be done. Actually they were the heralds who were conveying the light of Salvation to these savages. "Rubbish," says Fuenterrabia, who has just appointed a hen governor of a cornfield, "there will be hundreds of thousands after us." Perucho thinks that this is grossly exaggerated. There were but three or four thousand in Peru after so many years, precisely the right number to live a comfortable life. Only in this way would one enjoy it.

"I have a feeling that they're watching us," a man in the circle suddenly says. Everyone listens momentarily, the jungle is full of sounds, a fact that reassures the men a little. The steaming trees stand gloomily, nothing stirs at the jungle's edge. There, there he had seen something; he thought he had seen a man. Where, ask the others—they have seen nothing.

The two soldiers fighting for the best-protected place are attacking one another more vigorously now, shoving each other back and forth. "Here, from this crack on, you are forbidden to trespass." "Quiet," says Aguirre, and from then on the battle proceeds in silence. Aguirre commands them to be in constant readiness and to leave the arquebuses loaded. But the Spaniards still consider themselves comparatively secure because, as Perucho says, the jungle is singing. Danger would only arise from the silence.

Fuenterrabia is seriously engaged with giving out names and positions to the hens in the cages. His loaded arquebus is leaning beside him. Each of the hens was supposed to receive a whole corn-field, and once they had chickens, each chicken would get an Indian for a servant. Almost whimpering, he declares one of the hens his favorite and announces that he shall crown it. For this he takes a piece of silver wire, which he unravels from his powder horn, and working with painstaking precision, he starts to make a little crown with it. Fuenterrabia is exceedingly proud of his skillful work and responds morosely as the others jeer that the queen would be the first to be plucked and cooked. He tries the little crown out on the hen, but it is still too big and the hen just struggles, flutters and squawks.

Suddenly there is dead silence all around. ''I don't hear anything more,'' Perucho says. The river is divided by an island into two large arms of equal size, and now the Spaniards are in one arm trying to get to the middle of the river, as far removed from the riverbanks as possible. The jungle lies in horrible silence, maliciously still, the woodland waiting. Guzman gives the order to open fire, and the Spaniards shoot wildly into the foliage. Entire branches are torn off by the balls and tumble down. A man possessing only a sword has crept in terror beneath a blanket to protect himself. The whole raft is enveloped in gunpowder smoke. Shot after shot roars into the forest. But there is still no sound from within.

The horse has been roused by the shots and starts galloping about the raft, frightened and panicky, its forelegs fettered. It jumps over a row of gunners and slams into Flores' sedan, where Juan de Arnalte courageously throws himself in front of the horse, forcing it to retreat. Everything on board is in turmoil. A musket goes off, ripping to shreds half of the roof of bast in the middle of the raft. Luggage is lost and now drifts on the river. A sedan has tumbled over, and Arnalte holds Flores protectively in his arms; she is very frightened. Slowly calming down, the horse is pulled at by several men who are holding it to the deck. It stomps wildly about and kicks a man who goes flying several yards. The man rises but immediately sinks down again. Two men try to help him up, but they soon notice he is dead. "That's enough," Guzman says. The horse must leave the raft. Aguirre has examined the dead man and explains that he has died not from the horse's kick, but from a tiny dart that must have hit him an instant later. It was still sticking in the back of his hand. All at once the birds in the jungle start singing again, the sound passing through the woodland like a shock. One of the men on board remains sitting beneath his blanket, teased now by his comrades for his cowardice, and only after a great deal of persuasion does he appear, hesitantly. He sees Aguirre, Carvajal, and some of the others taking care of the dead man, and requests momentary silence to make sure that the sounds of the jungle had revived once again.

Dusk over the river

The raft has been tied to the shore, but the
jungle is so dense and the overhanging branches
jut out so far that first they had to hack a little
swathe amid the dripping leaves and twigs with
their knives. Over the smooth river the sun is
slowly sinking low. The waters are flowing sluggishly, without a sound. Millions of mosquitoes
are dancing in the night.
Hacking with their knives and swords the Spaniards carve a small clearing of just a few square
yards in the jungle. Creepers and foliage are im-
penetrably interwoven everywhere; the undergrowth is utterly impenetrable. Aguirre declares
his belief that what they are doing is a mistake.
It was irresponsible to abandon the only horse
they had merely because it easily shied and meant
danger for them. Your Honor should simply
keep in mind what a significant part horses have
played in the conquest of Mexico and Peru, for
the Indians had never seen such creatures before
and, therefore, entire armies had fled in
precipitous panic just because of some horses.
But Guzman pretends not to listen to him. He
apparently wants to accept this challenge of
power and is willing to show that he can hold his
own against Aguirre. Aguirre talks to him directly, but more so to all the men, and explains that
even if the horse were to be of no use in the near
future, that is to say, if the country of El Dorado
was still farther away than they had thought, it
certainly would provide a very important service

to the crew as a lifesaving article of food, since by that time all the provisions would have been used up. "Now that is enough, the horse must go," says Guzman, attempting to imitate Aguirre's own assured tone of voice. Aguirre hesitates for a few seconds as Perucho moves towards his musket, seemingly devoid of any ulterior motive. "Your Honor, the sun is going down," says Aguirre.

Seen from the raft. Without talking, and somehow touched, the men are standing on board gazing upon Clodoaldo, the stallion, who has been taken ashore. He has just enough space there to turn around once comfortably; everywhere around him he is enclosed by the jungle labyrinth. Evening's glow is spreading over the clouds in the sky. Like veils, the dancing gnats are waving. The horse paws the ground on its spot, flaring its nostrils as if it sensed something. From out of the jungle, plaintive cries of monkeys emerge. At the last moment before departure, Flores plucks a few leaves from a limb and places them in front of the horse. The tether is cut and the raft slowly frees itself from the land. It is a silent very sad scene. Slowly, in the red afterglow, the raft moves away from the horse. The horse is restless and whinnies. It is getting smaller and smaller and still one hears it whinnying. Very far away, we can still distinguish it as a small dark spot amid the green foliage, until distance and darkness swallow it up. "Come on, come on," Perucho's parrot continues crying in the darkness.

On the river, forenoon

The same river, the same islands, the same
jungle, the same heat, the same moldering, the
same clouds, as if a thunderstorm was approaching. Again we see the raft, drifting. The
river seems to have become even broader. All is
calm on board, with added space as well, we can
clearly see some gaps. Slowly the oarsmen steer
the craft in the middle of the current round a
long extended sandbar.

There, suddenly, behind a river bend, smoke appears over the jungle, we can clearly distinguish
it. At once the jungle is utterly still and threatening. Everything on board is instantly plunged into wild commotion. The Spaniards pile their luggage up as protective walls, and the curtains in
the sedans are carefully closed. The man without
a musket creeps beneath his blanket once again.

The Spaniards start firing some shots into the
stillness, and a few of them make a real racket
with their shields. The fright confronting the
stillness is great. Aguirre gives orders not to fire
too much, as they also must think about the gunpowder. There, all of a sudden, shrill cries from
the jungle, the voices of men. "Seems like hundreds of them," reckons Bermudez. "Now
they're in for it, we're going to give it to them,"
says Perucho.

View of the jungle. There, among the branches,
some Indians are already revealing themselves.
Wild and half-naked, they apparently wish to be

seen since they violently gesticulating for a moment, before vanishing again into the foliage. It seems as if they wanted to lure the Spaniards ashore.

On board, Aguirre asks for a green twig and waves it over his head. "Senneneh," scream the Spaniards, "Peace." "Jurua, jurau," the Indians call back, shrill and ecstatic from the jungle. "Meat, meat, there is meat swimming towards us," translates Baltasar. They are cannibalistic head-hunters, he says. Guzman gives the order to land, and the Spaniards fire feverishly to give themselves a clear spot for anchoring. When the raft is close to the land, the cries of the Indians stop as they withdraw noticeably into the shelter of the forest. Again, the jungle lies in utter stillness, full of danger and mystery.

After some waiting, when no attack is made from the dead silence of the forest, the Spaniards, who are ready for any sort of battle, get restless. At last, still with no leaf moving, Guzman orders five heavily-armored men to cautiously penetrate a little way into the woodland, in order to stake out the enemy. The men go ashore, and from a sandy place, they cautiously set out. Hacking away with knives, they must actually cut a swathe into the wildly-intertwined undergrowth to make any progress at all. Slowly the jungle swallows up the five.

View of the motionless jungle. For a while we continue to hear a rustling and a crackling and the hacking sounds of the knives. Gradually it dies away completely. Everyone on board is in a state of great suspense. All of the arquebuses are propped up on their forks, aimed towards the jungle. No more sound is coming, long waiting in absolute suspense. The river flows steadily on.

Suddenly a lone man, deeply disturbed, steps out from the swathe and stumbles directly over the sand into the water. Only then does he turn towards the raft which has been moored but a few yards upstream. The man carries no knife and has lost his weapons, holding nothing but his powder horn in his hands. The Spaniards on board begin to stir. "What is it?" asks Aguirre. But the man has lost his speech, horselike. He just makes a strange gesture towards the jungle and stumbles onto the raft.

Aguirre immediately sets out with twelve heavily-armed men. The traces of the troops who have cut a swathe in the jungle are distinctly visible. The cleared path makes a slight bend around a giant tree, then another one. Deep dusk and deathly-still silence. Aguirre hurries ahead of his men, sword in hand. The path suddenly stops, the jungle closed on all sides and overhead like the end of a tunnel, and there, everything is full of blood. All the leaves and twigs are red, and on the ground there is only a bloodied boot. There is nothing else, as if the men had dissolved into thin air. Profound threatening stillness oppresses the woodland.

On the raft

There is great excitement on board the raft. Aguirre has returned with his men, having brought back nothing but a boot filled with blood. Aguirre reports that he has searched everywhere, but it was simply inexplicable how the men could have disappeared without a sound, as if they had dissolved into nothing. The disturbed man from the vanguard slowly begins to talk again, and he haltingly reports that he had retreated briefly after noticing his powder had been lost. He did find it, hanging on a branch, and when he hurried after the others he could find nothing but blood. The blood still steamed with warmth, then without a doubt he dropped everything and fled. But they did not find any of his things, which is strange, adds Aguirre with a twist.

The Spaniards decide to infiltrate the jungle again with a stronger force, since disregarding the four men who could hardly be saved, provisions have become so scarce that they had to find some settlement or village. Once more Aguirre leads the trek, this time joined by Fuenterrabia and Juan de Arnalte. The troops penetrate the silent woodland.

A long look, roaming over the raft. There the men stand waiting with their arquebuses ready. Mosquitoes are making their wait torturous. The sedans stand motionlessly, with no movement behind their curtains. Carvajal, armed with a sword, takes shelter behind one of the bundles.

His tonsure is already woolly and overgrown. Muddy humus has gathered between two trunks on the edge of the raft. Upon looking closer, we notice that grass is beginning to grow there.

On the raft, nightfall

The crew of the raft continues to wait in constant readiness. Someone breaks the silence by saying he has heard something. The others listen, but they can't make anything out. Then there is a faint crackle and rustle from afar, indeed, coming closer rapidly. Then voices of Spaniards as well, and all of a sudden, Aguirre's troops are out in the open. They are carrying a man with them. When they draw nearer, it turns out to be Juan de Arnalte, who seems to be wounded in his chest.

"Nothing," says Fuenterrabia, "nothing to be found." He reports that suddenly, without the men noticing anything of the enemy whatsoever, Arnalte was wounded by an arrow. On board, Arnalte is carefully bedded on a mat. He asks for something to drink, and Flores quickly brings him a mug of water.

On the river, stormy day

The crew of the raft seems demoralized, and once more the gaps have widened. Guzman is laboring away in the outhouse with a tormented look on his face, no one saying a word. In the front of the raft, a few of the men are sleepily keeping vigil.

Inez and Flores are with the wounded Arnalte, who is lying there very weak. Inez carefully raises one of his arms and washes it with a clean cloth. Then she washes his face and Flores dries it. She does this with a great deal of loving care. Suddenly, shouting and commotion at the front of the raft; the men have caught sight of something. View from the front, along the river. Beyond a bend, on a sandbank, a raft is distinctly visible, and on it are Spaniards sitting in their armor. On board there is wild jubilation, for this is undoubtedly Orellana who was considered lost. They joyfully salute them with cannonballs fired skyward, but the Spaniards on board the other raft do not stir and very soon the jubilation ends. Upon coming closer we realize there are only dead people on board. Paralyzing fright creeps over the crew. The two rafts are attached to each other, and now we can clearly see that armored skeletons are sitting there without heads. Each of the helmets is stuck on a pole above the breastplates. And now we realize the horrible fact that each of the dead is holding his own head, shrunk to the size of an apple, in his skeletal outstretched hand. On the shriveled heads you can clearly distinguish facial traits, only the hair is much too long. The thick lips of the faces are sewn shut.

On the river, rain

The raft drifts along, as in a dream. Heavy warm rain is falling steadily down and the river is steaming. Nothing but a deep monotonous rushing sound. The river water is whitish-brown.

On the river, evening

Darkness has fallen and from the jungle there is hardly a sound. In the still-pale sky, huge bats are flying in an incomprehensible zigzag. Terror has spread through the raft and everyone is listening. Two small fireplaces continue to glimmer. The Spaniards are nibbling roots and soft-boiled bark, and eight men are sharing a fish that is a good nine inches long. Inez hands a drink to Arnalte who is lying apathetically. He takes very careful minute sips. In the middle of the vessel, under the half-destroyed bast roof, Guzman sits dining. His former cupbearer was one of the men who disappeared in the jungle, and so he has appointed another Spaniard who apparently does not suit him. Somewhat clumsily, the cupbearer serves him a large plate filled with cooked corn, and the men nearby are sniffing unobtrusively. Discreet glances are exchanged, and some can manage to suppress their rage only with difficulty. "Don't you have a plate for my piece of bark?" one of them says, but Guzman keeps eating good-humoredly, ignoring the inimical undertones. "El Dorado," shrieks Perucho's parrot.

Unnoticed by the oarsmen, the raft has come quite close to the edge of the jungle. All of a sudden, lianas are dangling on board. Simultaneously something shapeless and heavy splashes into the river with the sinister sound of a crocodile. Everyone on the raft is seized by fright, and all around is profound alluring blackness.

On the river, early morning

Some of the Spaniards are still sound asleep, Juan de Arnalte is lying in fever. On the sides of the raft, armed men are watching. "Hey, wake up," one of them says, slowly standing up in the middle of the raft, "I think our Emperor is dead." Slowly a few more arise in disbelief, and Aguirre joins them. "What?" he asks with astonishment.

We see Guzman closely now. He lies beneath a

blanket, and his eyes are widely dilated and his face is bloated. Around his neck his napkin has been tied and pulled tightly, blue streaks now observable there. "He is quite cold already," the Dominican says.

The men are all embarrassed, and each of them purposely avoids the question of who has done it. How should one bury him, that was the only question that mattered; whether by land or by water, and how should he be honored. He had been rather ill anyway, everyone could see that. The murder is accepted as a natural death, yet all are confused because no one knows who has done it. No one serves as informer, and the unconcerned try hard not to appear concerned, but this makes them even more conspicuous.

Sandy shore, jungle beyond

A nice tomb has been erected on shore, a well-polished wooden cross and an inscription. Smooth stones from the river are arranged around the mound. Some orchids bedeck it and a piece of candle is burning in a bowl. A few men in the background are digging in the sand for snails and crayfish, laboring weakly, and one has dug up turtle eggs from the sand which are attacked ravenously by the men. They eat them raw, as they are. Perucho is trying to fish from the raft with a rod, and several Spaniards are busy plaiting oyster-baskets with thin flexible tendrils.

Jungle, rain forest, twilight

The crew is working its way through labyrinths of lianas, searching for herbs and roots. With the tips of their swords they carefully dig up maniok roots and yucca plants from the soft moist soil. Parrots are shrieking and a laughing mockingbird bleats. A Spaniard proudly carries a killed snake and shows it to the others.

On the river, noontide

Spaniards are cooking their leather belts in a kettle, adding green herbs. With a spoon, Carvajal dispenses the last of the flour, which he had actually meant to reserve for the hosts. "We should have salt," someone complains. The kettle, closer. During the stirring, the single boot of the lost man soon rises to the surface. It is already soaked through and soft. The mood seems to be far better than the day before, some courage has seemingly returned to the men. Aguirre stands with Fuenterrabia and Bermudez at the front of the raft, gazing steadily outward. Can those be houses, those white things over there, asks Bermudez. Aguirre thinks he has been deceived, that it was merely the sand on a sandbank.

And up ahead, Bermudez timidly reflects, can that be a canoe with two people in it. Where, there's nothing to see, says Fuenterrabia. But there, indeed, on the very edge of the jungle is a boat. The camera studies the woodland fringe and, as a matter of fact, half hidden by tree limbs, a dugout canoe is afloat. Aguirre directs the two oarsmen to steer toward it quickly. Coming closer, we can recognize two Indians, a man and a woman, in a twenty-foot long dugout canoe. Having noticed the raft, they advance towards the Spaniards with oars dipping slowly, half surprised and half afraid, while the Spaniards are working wildly so the canoe can't get away. Now we see that both Indians are dressed only in a loincloth. The man is athletic and sinewy. The utmost excitement reigns on the raft. Once the canoe, timidly moved forward by the two Indians, is close enough, it is boarded by the Spaniards with a crude jolt. The two Indians are dragged aboard and Fuenterrabia tries to make a go at the woman at once. Aguirre stops him. Spaniards have jumped into the boat and triumphantly pull out several fish of three feet or more, which the Indians apparently have caught with bows and remarkably long arrows.

Before the Spaniards direct any questions to the

Indian, who seems to be rather small and of middle age, he begins talking slowly and with dignity, while held fast by several men. Baltasar answers him in a peculiar Indian dialect, and for a while the Indians talk with each other as if they were alone on board. He should translate at least, curses Perucho.

Baltasar and the strange Indian near him. Baltasar says, the man already knew from his forefathers that one day Sons of the Sun would come floating down the river, and they surely had come from afar with enormous hardships. He wanted to offer them whatever food he had and would prepare them a hammock, so at last they would get some rest. Yes, for a long time they had waited for the Sons of the Sun, since here, on this river, God had not finished his creation.

Aguirre wants to know what he was wearing around his neck on the string, and when he does not get an answer forthwith, Fuenterrabia rips the amulet off the Indian's neck. "Gold," he says, breathlessly. "Gold, gold," say the Spaniards. Wondrous and bewildered, the Indian is confronted by the Spaniards' greed. Where the country of El Dorado is, that is what the Spaniards want to know. But the Indian cannot give them any information as to where he got the gold from. From further downriver, the man indicates. This is too vague for the Spaniards, but the Indian is in no position to estimate the distance in leagues. Two days, he thinks, but fails to answer whether this is on foot or by boat. He says that he already knew about the raft, for the Indians further upriver had spread the news in advance that strangers were coming with thunder-cloud noise which they produced from tubes.

Carvajal, waiting impatiently all this time for his turn, asks the Indian if he had heard of our Savior Jesus Christ and of the True Word of God. The Indian is very confused and gives no answer. This, here, is a Bible with the Word of God, and they had come to carry God's Light into the darkness. While saying this he shows him a Bible. The Indian is dumbstruck and does not comprehend a thing. Yes, within this book is the Word of God, Carvajal insists. Deeply disturbed, the Indian picks up the Bible and puts his ear to it, listening. "It does not speak," he says and casts the Bible to the floor. Highly incensed, some Spaniards seize him at once and kill him on the spot. The Indian woman is injured defending herself and falls overboard. She drowns instantly. "Perhaps that was a mistake," says Aguirre.

On the river, rain

The current is pushing the raft on, giving it no other choice. Thundershowers pour down heavily and accelerate the decaying of the clothes. Already the Spaniards' harnesses have a thick layer of rust. A bundle of canvas is almost covered with mold. The Indians' pirogue has been tied to the rear of the raft, floating along with it.

Again, distinctly visible through the rushing of the rain, the woodland slips into silence. The Spaniards start to stir, but they obviously lack their former energy; many of them seem rather weak. Aguirre gives the order to shoot at regular intervals. The one cowardly man once more draws a blanket over his head, and the wounded Arnalte is covered with canvas as well. It looks as if he is slowly going downhill, he hardly responds anymore.

The man beneath the blanket is teased by his comrades, but apparently this does not bother him. He maintains his cowering posture beneath the blanket.

Under Aguirre's supervision, Bermudez has poured the last of the corn from an almost-empty bag into a bowl, and under the hungry eyes of all, the corn is dispensed kernel by kernel, counted out carefully. Some stray gunshots still rumble across the water. The arquebuses also get their ration. It is quite a laconic scene. No one says a word, just one of them counting the kernels. A man stands entranced beneath the cover of a bale, mutely recounting his kernels. Bermudez calls out for Manrique, but the man underneath the blanket does not answer. An arquebus shooter nudges him with his foot, but still he does not stir. Then Perucho comes over to make sure. He lifts up the blanket a bit, and beneath it sits the man named Manrique with his head bent back, looking upwards with a glassy ecstatic gaze. He is totally stiff and dead. Some of the men refuse to believe it, but they find a small dart with a tiny cotton puff sticking in his neck. He could have been hit only in instant when he threw the blanket over himself, says Perucho. He had the impression, that something had come flying in like a shadow, but he had not seen where it came from, nor did he have an impression from having seen it directly at all.

The terror on the raft increases, and the Spaniards make a lot of noise so that they won't have to listen to the stillness. They are shooting about wildly, even making a racket with the pots and pans. We look at the raft from a distance. The powder clouds mingle with the steam from the warm rain, and from the raft comes an infernal noise. The dusky jungle stands quite taciturn in the pouring rain. On the raft Perucho's parrot starts to scream.

Indian settlement by the river

Seen from the raft. All the men have crowded together at the front end of the raft, staring with fascination at an Indian settlement up ahead. The houses, about a hundred of them, stand close together on top of thin poles several yards above the ground, and for the first time we see a free spot on shore, and a clearing. The buildings are airy and their side walls consist of fluttering bast mats, the roofs are covered with palm fronds. Several canoes have been drawn ashore and fish nets are lying about to dry. Over the village huge clouds of smoke are rising up into the sky, and at the edge of the clearing some storehouses are burning completely ablaze. No man anywhere in sight, no sound, only the ghostly crackling of the fire. Up on the patio of the nearest house, hammocks in the wind lashed to the posts of the house are rocking gently in the wind.

The Spaniards do not fire any shots, they merely let themselves drift ever so cautiously near the pillared settlement, allowing the raft to run aground on the sand quite delicately, without tying it up at all. Aguirre signals his men to wait. For a long time the Spaniards wait in front of the abandoned village. They are apparently afraid of a trap. Now we recognize the open square, which has been kept free by the houses in the center of the settlement. From there, a path leads upward into the jungleland. Some fish nearby are hanging on a line to dry.

After a long silent wait, Aguirre whispers an order to Fuenterrabia to guard the raft with five men. At the head of his gang of wild and starved men, he then storms straight into the settlement. While running, the Spaniards fire shots from their arquebuses, wave their swords and storm forward, shouting. They search the first houses in no time and then stand back from the burning storehouses.

A Spaniard cries out from a house that he has found a pot filled with food that was still quite warm. The others storm this house yelling. We see a Spaniard try to catch a wild turkey in an enclosed square. At last, overwhelmed with greed, he flings himself on top of the bird. Two men rush towards the jungle path where the dried fish are hanging but, all of a sudden, the jungle is raining arrows. One of the pair is wounded instantly above the eye, and only with some difficulty can the others withdraw. "There they are, in the jungle," one of them screams, and Aguirre rushes ahead with about ten men. All fire madly into the woodland, but the Indians are invisible, only shooting whole clouds of arrows. The Spaniards slowly withdraw, the provisions being their lone concern.

Now we behold a Spaniard kneeling by a track in the sand in the open square greedily licking the ground. Others come along. "Salt!," they scream, filled with ecstasy. Tears stream down the face of a Spaniard who now licks the ground. Suddenly, a strange scene. Like a vision, Inez in her most beautiful long royal gown of purple velvet, steps upright across the square past the burning storehouses. Her face is waxen and her hair is flowing down to her shoulders. The men licking the ground glance up, rigid with surprise. Unable to trust their eyes, they do not move. Inez walks directly towards the jungle fringe like a queen, and a moment later she disappears into the dark glade. "Captain, sir!" someone calls now to Aguirre, but no one dares to go near the jungle. The path lies silent and dusky, swallowed up by the jungle after just a few feet. For a long time our gaze remains fixed to the path.

Indian settlement, towards evening

Almost all the Spaniards are gathered on the raft where they have accumulated their modest catch. They have placed a turkey in one of the empty chicken coops. Whispering, the men are talking about Inez. Bermudez tells Aguirre in a low voice that those five men left on board would not broach the matter but, rather, would keep their mouths shut. Inez had left the moment that Flores had gone with the monk to find fresh water for the sick Arnalte, but, in his opinion, she was raped by the men. Anything was possible with Fuenterrabia and his gang. We shall see whether she can be found again, says Aguirre, but avoids clearing up the matter fully. Flores is sitting with the wounded Arnalte, apparently deeply shocked. She hardly moves at all, and by her face she seems to be thirty.

Seven heavily armed men are coming from a gap in the jungle across the open square, towards the raft. Two of the men carry the line with the dried fish in between them. They were not able to detect anything, Perucho reports, as they had cautiously penetrated into the jungle for about half a league but had not uncovered any natives. Then the path had branched out into two smaller paths, and first they had followed the one, then the other. But they had returned without delay, having been afraid of traps. One of the men, he would not say who, had been seized with mortal terror because of the profound stillness in the forest. They had not found any trace of Inez de

Atienza, not even a footprint.

"Men," says Aguirre, "our number must not be reduced any further." The men around him are depressed because of the deserted place. Remnants of the storehouses are still glowing in the background.

The Spaniards have kindled some fires on the sand in front of the raft and are busy preparing a big meal. They all sit expectantly for the food to be distributed, and on the open square facing the jungle, twin sentries are keeping vigil. Judging from the way the Spaniards have arranged things, they must feel relatively secure.

A man is sitting in the sand somewhat removed from the others, talking softly and urgently to another man. The two, a little closer. The soldier sitting with his back to the crowd of Spaniards tries to persuade the other that it would be better to leave the squadron in order to return to Peru by land somehow with a fair amount of provisions. He had had enough by now, this undertaking would only mean the certain perdition of them all.

Sitting with his crew, Aguirre starts listening and subtly directs his attention towards the discontented man. The latter has talked himself into a passion and raises his voice carelessly. It would still be preferable to put him on trial in Peru for having disobeyed orders, but it should be possible to keep marching alongside the river, that is to say, during the night, since during the day they would have to hide.

Aguirre very cautiously nudges Fuenterrabia who starts listening as well. "The man is a head taller than me," he says in a low voice, "but that may change." Fuenterrabia has understood. He casually rises, taking his sword with him as if only incidentally. Apparently having nothing in mind, he walks near the soldier sitting with his back to him and who is just explaining to his comrade, by means of a rough sketch, how many days, march they would need from here. "Five, six, seven," he counts. Fuenterrabia has stopped behind him and is raising his sword. The man to whom this plan is being explained doesn't dare say anything in his terror. He just sits there rolling his eyeballs around, twisting his face into a horrible grimace, trying to tell his partner to turn around. But the discontented man has talked himself into such a passion that he continues counting, oblivious to the rolling of the eyes. "Eight, nine," he says. At this moment, Fuenterrabia cuts off his head from behind with an awful blow. "Ten," the head still says, already in flight.

With the entire camp paralyzed by surprise, Aguirre rises. "I am the Great Betrayer," he says. "There must be no one greater." A long silence ensues, no one dares to move. "Men," says he, "I, Aguirre, am the Wrath of God." Then he commands Bermudez, the scrivener, to come forth. In front of everyone he now dictates a document. Whoever removes himself even mentally from this doomed troop shall be cut up into ninety pieces, which shall be trampled upon to such an extent that the walls might be painted with them. Whoever eats one kernel of corn more than his share shall be imprisoned for one hunrdred and fifty-five years. He who would let himself drift downstream to act out the role of his own fate, however, shall be assured of riches unlike anyone has ever seen at any time before. If he, Aguirre, willed the birds to drop dead from the trees, the birds shall drop dead from the trees. Upon reaching El Dorado, he and his daughter shall establish a new Very Pure Dynasty. This was the Course of History, and already it had been chosen for this country, irrevocably.

Aguirre asks for the finished document and signs it: Aguirre, the Wrath of God.

The men are duly impressed and shout with joy. Even Carvajal displays great enthusiasm. Fuenterrabia and Perucho fire their arquebuses into the sky and rejoice. The buildings are standing atop their stilts and some hammocks are gently rocking in the wind. The joyful shouts are echoed by the dead-silent woodland.

Flores is sitting on the raft next to Arnalte whose health has deteriorated visibly, and wondering, first she looks at Arnalte then at Chimalpahin, the Inca. The latter is staring serenely and restfully at some clouds puffing up on the twilit horizon.

On the river, lower course of the Amazon

The river has widened immensely now, sometimes measuring about six miles, then again it is divided into a great number of intertwined branches.

Islands overgrown with jungle appear more and more frequently. Entire formations of trees with their soil and roots pointing skyward are floating like islands towards the sea. There the raft is drifting.

At first glance we notice that the situation on the raft has degenerated considerably. The gaps are wide and there are only about twenty men left. Some of them are lying wracked with fever, and Juan de Arnalte can hardly breathe. The whole raft is rotting, and no one tries to save it anymore. The tuft of grass between the two logs has grown markedly. Ahead of the raft, the river splits into several branches, and the two oarsmen are unable to decide which to take. At last, taking Aguirre's advice, they decide to take the widest one, on the extreme left. The raft drifts slowly on and, beyond a bend, the branch of the river winds up in the jungle. Slowly the raft drifts towards the end of the blind alley. We realize now that this branch of the river continues on through the jungle, that all of the trees are standing in the water. Very depressed, the Spaniards on board let themselves float close to the trees without doing anything.

Aguirre assigns Perucho the task of taking the canoe, which is still bound to the raft, out amongst the trees to see how far they would have to go to come to the open river again. If necessary, they would cut down the trees en route to get through, for it was almost impossible to get the raft into another branch of the river against the current.

Perucho sets out with three men, we are with

him. Slowly the canoe penetrates into the dusk of the jungle. The oars dip quietly, and the long slender canoe proceeds slowly among the huge tree trunks. Lianas are dangling down touching the boat. Far away a jaguar roars. Leaves the size of a wagon wheel are floating on the water with turned-up edges, huge water lilies amongst them. Brooding dusk in the woodland. All around, the staring of flowers, the ardor of orchids. The men in the canoe are very quiet. Monkeys begin to chatter above them, single leaves are fluttering down and start to float. The men are crouching in terror and only row lightly. The water stretches out through the jungle endlessly.

Return journey on the blind river branch

We now spot the raft on the jungle fringe, and all of the men on board are trying desperately to pull the raft backwards against the current while holding on to the overhanging limbs. Grabbing the limbs with their hands, they lean back with all their might and thus move the vessel almost imperceptibly upstream. To the rear of the raft, four men are working with long poles with which they poke the ground. Aguirre is amongst them, working indefatigably, unflinchingly. He pays no attention to the mosquitoes which are torturing him. He pokes his pole vertically into the ground and leans against it until it slowly becomes diagonal and sinks into the muddy water almost up to his hands. Then he pulls it out again.

Even Flores and Baltasar with his chained hands try to pull themselves forward with the branches, and the monk, who looks ever more savage, is working with them as well. His hair has grown bushy and has gotten all matted like boiled sheep's wool.

We now observe the raft somewhat further along, at a place where the jungle recedes several feet and leaves a small, sandy space on the bank. Except for the four men still punting to the rear, everyone else has gotten off to drag the raft along with ropes. They have placed the ropes over their shoulders and are leaning forward, almost horizontally, their feet planted into the sandy ground. With awesome effort they gain ground, step by step. All of them utterly exhausted, they just stagger along.

This unspeakable labor has prevented them from noticing that no sound has come from the jungle in quite some time. All at once there is a strange rustle, and the first man bolts upright with considerable strain, an incredibly long arrow in his chest. The man, closer. He drops the rope and calmly grabs the arrow with both hands, the tip of which is sticking out of his back. The arrow is sticking up about six feet in front, pointing diagonally into the air. The man calmly measures the arrow with his eyes. "The long arrows have come into fashion," he says. Then he collapses and dies.

In a panic, all of the Spaniards drop their ropes and jump on board. Instantly the raft begins to drift indolently once again. The men fire about wildly, completely mad. The arquebusmen are working like crazy, shooting volleys into the jungle which is moving past slowly like before. Amid the thunder of guns, the raft is drifting back the same way in bluish smoke. At last Aguirre succeeds in bringing the raft to a halt with a hook, attaching it to a strong branch.

Amazon delta, about one hundred miles upland

The river has branched out more and more, and we behold a vast region of parting and rejoining tributaries. In the midst of a damp stifling steam, the raft floats along between two islands. Rain falls at a distance, the walls of water streaming down from the sky as gray as glass.
Most of the men on board the raft are lying down, scarcely one of them having strength enough to look ahead, due to exhaustion, sickness and hunger. Resignation has spread on deck. Juan de Arnalte is dying, and Flores kneels with the monk alongside him to pray. Aguirre has gotten a rash on his neck, but he is the only one who seems unresigned. He walks up and down the raft, accomplishing most of the work himself.
A Spaniard suddenly arises. ''Don't you hear

drumming?", he says. There is a slight commotion amongst the others. All of them strain to hear something, yet no one can hear a thing. "Yes," says another one, suddenly. "Don't you hear?" Ta-room toom-toom. He indicates the rhythm with his finger. "You are mad," says Fuenterrabia. "Come on," Perucho's parrot says.

On a sandbank, the jungle beyond

The raft has been tied, and Perucho fires a single shot into the stillness of the jungle before him. "We are being watched. When it gets quiet, someone will have to die." But, nevertheless, the few Spaniards who have survived are so starved and sick that they go ashore. Some of them lean on sticks out of sheer exhaustion and start searching the sand for something edible. A few of them penetrate into the jungle, and one is so exhausted that he creeps on all fours into the woodland.

To the rear of the raft, Carvajal and Chimalpahin sink a crudely made fish net into the water. They are both pensive and mum.

Flores is sitting near them, dreamlost, singing to herself in a very low voice. She sings a song:

Fish are filling up the nets,
Pike and perch.
Our Noble Host has wine and such
So good and more than much.

Fish are filling up the nets,
Bass and butt.
Our Noble Host has wine and such
So good and more than much.

Fish are filling up the nets,
Carp and trout.
Our Noble Host has casks of beer
So very good and stout.

How these things are bountiful fare,
How they are beyond compare!

How these things are made to please,
How they make for mutual ease!

How these things are here in masses,
Just for a while and then it passes!

Sandbank, towards evening

Some luggage from the raft has been brought
ashore, and a small smoky fire has been lighted.
The Spaniards slowly emerge from the jungle one
by one, most of them carrying some yucca plants

or other herbs. One of them has even shot a big bird of paradise. Apathetically they crouch around the fire and, while eating part of the meal raw, begin to prepare the food. After a long silent spell, one of them asks of the stillness, "Where is Pedro?" "Yes," says another, "Empudia is missing."

Aguirre orders three men to look for Empudia, Fuenterrabia amongst them. At these trees, he points out, is where Empudia crept into the jungle quite some time ago. The three men penetrate into the forest, making their way forward, bending the branches apart. They come across an enormous moldering tree which lies there defeated by creepers. And there, on the ground, a horrifying image. The man named Empudia is on all fours on the ground, stiff and dead, his mouth still filled with palmshoots, upon which he had been grazing like an animal. Empudia has a tiny blowgun dart in his neck, and seems to be completely rigid. "Come, quickly!" shouts Fuenterrabia filled with horror, now firing his arquebus into the foliage. Twigs are crackling, there is a rustling sound, and the Spaniards burst through the branches. All of them become paralyzed with fright. "Baltasar," we suddenly hear Flores cry from the sandbank.

The Spaniards come creeping out of the jungle and run to the sandbank. There lies the raft, and in the middle of the river Chimalpahin is slowly rowing away with the canoe. He does not turn around, since he knows he is already beyond the reach of their guns. He works the paddle with his two hands tied and, utterly calm, he disappears behind a densely overgrown island. "Now he dies alone," says Aguirre. Far away, evening is drawing near, and walls of rain are towering over the river.

Then Perucho notices that a bundle of luggage is floating on the water, that the water level has risen. This is a flood, this was because of the rain, he says. Yes, the water had been up to here a couple of hours ago, now it has almost reached the fireplace. "Men," says Aguirre, "I feel the ocean."

Amazon delta, about sixty miles upland

The same picture as often seen before. Only twelve men are still alive on board. Two corpses are lying wrapped in blankets. Apparently one of the dead is Juan de Arnalte, but no one has any strength or energy left to bury the dead, or to throw them overboard. Almost everyone is sick and totally degenerate, a piteous sight. Carvajal talks to the men and tells them to show repentance, for their sins had led them deep-down to the sea. The tide was growing steadily stronger, and they would drift three leagues forward and then two back again. That was a clear sign from Heaven. "Quiet, monk!" Aguirre thunders at him. They had not found El Dorado, it was just a delusion perhaps, but now it was time to make new plans.

91

A sudden outcry from the front of the raft. "A brigantine, certainly, there is a Spanish ship." It passes through the raft like a shock. Now we are looking across the river at the jungle where, indeed, a brigantine is sitting in the tree tops, about one hundred yards upland. Upon coming closer we see that the sails are tattered and creepers are growing round the main mast; it is like a ghostly vision. The men on board think they are dreaming. That wasn't a Spanish boat, how could it be, it is utterly impossible, argues Perucho. The others are dumbstruck. Those with a fever sink into their dreams. Someone should investigate this, says Aguirre, while the raft is stationary. Judging by the marks on the trees, it did look as though the tide sometimes rose about twelve fathoms until it went over the tops of the trees, and if the water sank afterwards once more, it could happen that a ship would get caught. He will convince himself of this.

Aguirre sets out with Perucho and Carvajal, but Perucho follows behind hesitantly. The three of them work their way through the jungle and soon reach the brigantine, the keel does not even reach to the boggy floor of the jungle. The men try climbing a giant tree overgrown with creepers, but already Carvajal is too weak and lags behind. Perucho and Aguirre reach the deck of the boat which is densely grown over with creepers, soil and foliage. Perucho touches the wood he is standing on ever so timidly, and hardly dares to step on it. Moldy sails are flapping lazily in the wind and moldy ropes are dangling from the decks. It is a ghostly scene. This cannot be, this is not a Spanish ship, says Perucho. Aguirre tries to find something on board, but the boat is completely empty.

Long view from the boat, circling the jungle. As far as the eye can see, clusters of tree after tree, tree tops like an unknown sea. Some solitary mud-flowing branches of the lazy river amongst them, an unimaginable sight.

On the raft

Aguirre has returned with his two men and, at first glance, the men rise up against him belligerently. This is enough by now, says Fuenterrabia, all of them have now had enough, they will not go on. Aguirre quickly takes off himself and makes his way towards the raft, utterly resolved, while Fuenterrabia tries to stop him. But he himself is not so sure of the men behind him, either. Aguirre warns his men not to let themselves be deceived by hallucinations, thereby getting so confused; he had convinced himself with his own eyes and hands that the boat really existed. Indeed, they had not reached El Dorado, and the sea was very close, but now the time had come to make even bolder plans. They would — and he was hereby calling on everyone to follow him — build a brigantine upon reaching the sea, and then they would sail northward, up to the Isle of Trinidad, to wrench the Spanish colony there away from the local governor. From there — and never again would the world witness a greater treachery — they would take all of the land from the undeserving Pizarro and Cortez, for now they wanted to have power over the whole of New Spain and New Andalusia. A great New and Pure Dynasty would emerge mighty in the world. "The Wrath of God has spoken!" cries Aguirre, "Who is for me?"

Four men stand beside Aguirre only hesitantly, Perucho among them. Aguirre realizes that he will not have the majority on his side any more. "Flores, come here!", he cries, "Thou shalt not witness this disgrace." Flores advances towards her father and he stabs her on the spot. Sighing, Flores sinks to the ground. "Monk," says Aguirre, "do not forget to pray, lest God's end be uncomely." The two parties immediately begin to fight, a swift and savage melee during which the raft frees itself from the bank. Some of the feverish men can no longer partake in the fighting. The raft drifts away as we realize that several people on board have been wounded, and Aguirre's head is bleeding. Then the fight is suddenly over. We cannot tell why.

Amazon delta

For a long time we watch the raft drift distantly on the river, without any pilot whatsoever. It first moves backwards for awhile, then it comes to a standstill and starts floating forward. It is very quiet, and the water is hardly flowing any more.

Mouth of the Amazon, open sea

We see a broad tributary flow into the open sea, and hundreds of small and smaller islands are lying before it. Heavy clouds, towering up into the sky. The raft is slowly drifting between two islands overgrown with jungle, and further away we see the waves of the sea. The raft is pilotless, and from a distance we recognize several corpses piled up on the tree trunks. The two sedans are silhouetted against the horizon, and only a small part of the bast roof is still intact. Across the vast surface of the water a cry is echoing. "El Dorado," Perucho's parrot screams.

Long, long view. Then, when the raft has reached the open sea, and drifts out amongst the long-drawn waves, the camera turns to the land with an ineffable view over the islands. Above the jungle, pillars of smoke are rising everywhere. Bonfires are lighted in the jungle. From the profound silence, drums begin to sound from afar, accompanied by intoxicated flutes. Rain clouds are towering high.

There it lies, the Sad Country.

Every Man for Himself and God Against All

For Lotte Eisner
("The Oarsman sat quietly and praised the
journey.")

Characters

Kaspar
The Unknown Man
Weickmann, Shoemaker
Cavalry Captain
Hiltel, Prison Guard
Mrs. Hiltel
Julius, Hiltel's Son
Daumer
Fuhrmann, Parson
Kaethe, Daumer's Housekeeper
Lord Stanhope
Hombrecito, Indian
The Little King
Mozart
and others

Small, half-obscured room, Kaspar's prison

There is a deep gloom. From out of the darkness of the picture dawn arises, and in the first dawning we see Kaspar. He snorts and makes animal noises. Over the persistent and unfriendly dawn the titles appear.

Somewhat more light. The room is dusky, hardly bigger than Kaspar when he lies stretched out. Cool, side walls rather irregular, as in a cellar, flattened straw on the floor. At about shoulder's height, if one stood up in the tiny room, there are two small rectangular windows side by side, each only as big as a book, and scarcely any light penetrates the interior from outside. It is only from a few exceedingly thin crannies that we see how the windows are sealed from outside with stacked wooden logs. To Kaspar's left, two little wooden horses whose feet are rooted in a small plank beneath little wheels. Besides the horses an additional toy, a small somewhat crudely-carved dog, also on wheels. All of the animals are painted white. Some colored ribbons are tied around the animals in disorderly fashion, they are loose because Kaspar doesn't know what a knot is. Further on is an empty jug of water, and in a small spot where the straw has been carefully cleared away there are two slices of bread, still untouched. To Kaspar's right, just a hand's breadth away from his hip, is a wooden lid that closes at floor level, an earthenware pot is underneath it. To Kaspar's rear we can discern the outline of a low door, but Kaspar shows interest only for his jug and his animals.

Kaspar is sitting in the room in a strange position of complete equanimity, his feet outstretched away from his body and his legs flat on the ground, even the backs of his knees are completely flattened out. From the knees downward his legs are covered with a coarse woolen blanket, but through the blanket the outline of his naked toes is visible. Kaspar sits on the floor in a peculiar half-crouched posture, twisted up somewhat, and when he turns a bit to the side we notice that he is tied to the ground by the waistband of his leather pants. Kaspar is dressed otherwise only in a loose shirt and suspenders. From the manner of his movements we perceive that he doesn't even have the will to sit erect, that the state of being tied to the ground doesn't bother him in the least, and that he apparently accepts this as part of his anatomy. Kaspar radiates an animal's neglect.

Kaspar nestles amid the ribbons of his toy horses, yet he doesn't move them away from their places. Then he lifts the jug, putting it to his mouth, but there is no more water in it. For a long, long time Kaspar holds the jug up high by his mouth, as if after awhile the water would start to come by itself.

Now, once the titles are over, Kaspar's voice begins to emerge, it is intense but hesitant, piercing us through and through.

Kaspar's voice: I want to say myself how hard it be for me. There, where I was always lokked in, in this prison, it seemed there wel to me, becos I knew naught of this world, and so long as I was lokked in and never seen no human being. I had two wood orses and a dog, and with these I always played, but I cannot say if I played all the day or the week, I knew not when was a day or a week, and I wanto describe, how it looked like in the prison, there was straw in it. And my trousers were open behind, there I taken off the lid, and there I relieved nature. And besides, there was nothing there, nor a stove, niether. The toy orses I moved not from their place, becos I knew not that you can move them, and the ribbons fell off becos I knew no knot. I knew naught that there was other humans, never have I perceived one of those, never a thunderstorm, neither. Since my mouth become dry, I very often take the little jug in my hand and place it to my mouth very very long, but water never came out, I waited some time, whether water came out soon, becos I knew not that it must be filled, whilst I was asleep.

A long, long time was I lokked in there, I knew no other. I knew naught from the world, becos never I had seen a man, never a house, a tree, or hears a sound, of speech I knew naught at all. Also, it never came into my mind that I should get up, since I was tied to the ground. That there come new bread and that what I made was cleaned away, surprised me not, becos I thought it come by itself.

I always been jolly and con-tented, becos naught never hurt me not; and thus I did all the time of my life, until the man come, and teached me how to copy, but I knew not what I did writ.

Behind Kaspar the door opens and the Unknown Man comes in, Kaspar is unfrightened, unsurprised and in complete equanimity, letting everything happen to him. The man has a stool with him which he sets down across Kaspar's legs. He places a sheet of paper upon it, puts a pencil into Kaspar's hand, and, approaching him from the back, closes his fist around Kaspar's hand and guides it.

Kaspar's voice: When now the man come for the first time to me; but I heard not how he come, at once, he has placed a little chair in front of me, and ther he brings a paper and a piece of pencil. All at once the man grips me by the hand and puts the pencil in my hand.

The Unknown Man doesn't utter a word. After a while he lets Kaspar scribble on his own, but Kaspar draws only meaningless zigzag lines. The Unknown Man defines the letters with Kaspar's fingers and, slowly, Kaspar begins to imitate the characters. We see quite clearly and somewhat closer now that he is writing a name: Kaspar Hauser.

The Unknown Man commences teaching Kaspar words, saying "Horse" several times, enunciating very intensely. Kaspar pauses, listening for a long time. The Unknown Man grabs the little horse, and guides Kaspar's left hand to the horse. He rolls the little horse back and forth. "Horse," says Kaspar, touching the horse. The Unknown Man makes him repeat this several times, again guiding his right hand to write. "Remember

102

this," he says. "Remember this," says Kaspar. "Remember this, repeat this, then you will get such a beautiful horse from Father as well," says the Unknown Man. ''From Father,'' says Kaspar. The Unknown Man cautiously disengages himself from Kaspar and disappears into the background; Kaspar is by himself once more. It is getting somewhat darker.

Kaspar's voice: Then he has learnt me this, and guided my hand, and the man was behind me, and then I made it myself' and I made it alone, this writing, for a long time, like this, and remembered all that he said, and from that time I knowed how the orses are called. And the man was away again, and I know not where he were, but he left the chair and the paper, there I notice the man for the first time, I saw him not, becos he was behind me, and how this man placed the chair I left it, for I was not clever yet to remov the chair when I layed down, and when I wake up again, then I drank the water again, and ate the bread, then first I begun to write, and then, that I finished the writ I took the orses and arrayed them again, then I did with the orse likewise, as he had showed me, and roled so hard that my own ears were hurting. . .

At first daylight. Kaspar rolls the horses back and forth, pressing down hard on the left hand side, rolling them over the wooden lid at last. There is a loud hollow noise. Kaspar utters loud gleeful cries, like an animal. Behind him the door opens, and a furious blow with a wooden log hits Kaspar on his elbow. Kaspar is astonished beyond measure, his breathing stops with the fright. The door slams hastily again, and the sound of steps two at a time hurriedly withdrawing.

Kaspar's voice: . . .then this man came and beat me with this stick, and hath hurt me so much that I weeped quietly, so that my tears fell down, and hath hurt me on my right elbow, and I knew not where from this blow came forth, all at once, and I knew not what a blow is, neither. There I keeped very quiet, becos it give me a lot of pain, and so I arrayed my orses and put the ribbons down softly: that I know not mysell how softly I done it; and then, when I relieved my nautre, I put the lid away very softly, and from my straw, on which I sat and layed, I never could go away, becos, first of all I knew not how to walk, and secondly I could not go away. It was as if something was keeping me there, and I never though to mysell that I wanted to leave, or that I was lokked in.

Dawn remains. We can see that Kaspar is sleeping deeply, keeping the stool at the same place over his knees. The Unknown Man enters by the door, unties Kaspar's waistband from the floor and dresses him with jacket and boots. He begins to lift the still half-sleeping Kaspar. Seen only from behind, he takes a handkerchief and binds Kaspar's hands. Then he props him up on his legs, supporting him at the same time, and leans him against the next wall. Kaspar allows his hands to slip down from him, he has no idea that he is supposed to hold on. With his hip bent forward a bit, the Unknown Man presses Kaspar against the wall so that he doesn't fall, and places Kaspar's folded hands, which are bound tightly around the wrists, around his neck from behind. Then he takes Kaspar and carries him off, piggyback.

Kaspar's voice: Now came this man and lifted me up from my sleepe and dressed me with a jacket and boots, and when he dressed me, he hath put me to the wall, and hath taken twoo hands and put them on the neck. When he borne me out of the prison he hath had to bow' and hath borne me up over a little mountain . . .

Lonely hill, big tree-tops

Dusk. The unknown Man makes a great effort to climb the back of the hill with Kaspar, some distance away from us. Beautiful grass, a few broad and billowy old beech trees on the crest of the hill. Over the trees a formidable storm threatens from the skies far away, above a forest flaring up twice.

Kaspar's voice: . . .there I froze so much, becos I never had the air, and such a frightful odor hath attacked me, that it hath hurt me very much. Then I started to crie, then the man hath sayed and indicated, I should stop, or I get no orses. . .

Closer. On top of the hill, between the trunks of the beeches, the Unknown Man puts Kaspar down, that is, face down to the ground. The grass is fermenting from the rain. He unties the handkerchief which is twisting Kaspar's wrists together too tightly. Exhausted, Kaspar sleeps. He awakens but doesn't move because he has never been lying down before. The Unknown Man grabs him around his chest from behind and stands him on his legs. Using his legs, he pushes Kaspar's legs forward and makes the first attempts at walking with him.

Kaspar's voice: . . .but I cannot say wither the mountain hath lasted long, becos I went asleep. And when I wake up, there I was lying on the earth, and was lying on my face, and there it smelled frightfully, and everything pained me. When I awoke, I turned my head, there the man will have sawn me, and hath come and lifted me, and hath learned me how to walk, hath pushed away one foot after the other with his foot, becos at the beginning he hath guided me on tween arms and held me round my chest, becos I knew not what was a step and what was walking. Since walking was so hard on me and all hath hurt me so much, there I weeped and sayed, "Orse, orse," with this I would say to bring me back to where I was lokked in. . .

The Unknown Man puts the obviously exhausted Kaspar down, slowly it is starting to get dark, and a soft rain is falling. The Unknown Man keeps prompting Kaspar with the sentence, "I want to be such a one orse rider, as my father hath been. Several times Kaspar repeats after him haltingly, "Su a rider". The Unknown Man lifts

Kaspar up again and, mercilessly, continues walking.

Kaspar's voice: . . .from above there was a soft weeping and I sayed orse, with this I would say, stop, there I knew not that this was rain, and that the rain stops when it will. And there my feet hurt so much that I really cannot say how, and there he giv me some water and bread, and he keept behind me, so that I shall not see his face never, and when I ate that up, I surely made eight steps of my own, but the pains wouldn't stop. Then it grew dark and then I fell asleep at once, becos I had made my farthest way alone.

It is growing dark. Deep night falls.

Way to town, dreamlost images

It is still dark when we hear Kaspar's voice again. He speaks the first sentences into the utter darkness. Then it grows light, overly-light. On an overly-light green we recognize in a brief, but very distinct flash, single stalks of grass.

Kaspar's voice: . . .Upon my awake, for the first time I noticed, what was there, I seed things which before I never did know of. There was a Green and a Grass, and it hath hurt mine eyes, it was so bright. . .

It becomes glaringly bright, as if one were looking into the sun, all is flooded with an overly-light white.

Kaspar's voice: . . . then we went away, then
mine feet hurt so much. The way there I do
not remember where we went. There was a
path with tracks of wheels, there were needles
from pine trees on my coat, blown there,
there the forest was sick. . .

A sandy path; we see in a flash the trail of a
horsecart. Pine needles on a jacket sleeve. The
pine trees standing scantily in the light, moving
slightly, unreal.

Kaspar's voice: . . .there was a cornfield, there it
was so light, that hurt me, and crickets
screamed, and I thought they were humans
screaming there. . .

A wheat field whose borders are not visible, as if
they were electrically lit in glaring light. Overhead it seems to be like high electric voltage. A
borderless, unreal, mechanical, senseless field of
wheat. We hear the sharp chirping of the crickets
screaming ever louder, screaming all at once like
human beings, shrill to the ears.

Kaspar's voice: . . .there I sayed "be rider", with
this I wanted to say the Screaming hurts, that
I be tired of all this walk. Then there was a
mountain, a farmer, a dog, and I knew of
naught what they were. . .

The screaming of the crickets continues, like a
human choir. In very bright light we see, as if
leafing through, a hill and a brook in a valley.
The brook is narrow and completely grown over
with grass. Willow stumps stand alongside the
winding waterway. An old ash tree at a distance.
The dog bites his raging pains into the bark of a
tree. The farmer has a shotgun with him. The
images flicker out into brightness.

Kaspar's voice: . . .there was a woman and a
    water, there was a cattle by the water, and a
    boy was standing on it, that I was all afright-
    ened, I seed he was barefoot. . .
We see a woman stop short with her wash on a
broad calm creek, she pauses, dreamlost and
semi-erect, looking directly at us, motionless. In
the background, a bit downstream, an ox is
drinking, standing there in equanimity. On his
back he carries a boy of about five years who
stands upright on bare feet; he is holding a stick
which he beats against the flanks of the ox very
softly. He looks at us, the spectators unflinchingly. Brightnesses flicker across the screen like a
thunderstorm. The crying of the crickets stops.

The Tallow Square in the Town of N., Kaspar's
birth

Townhouses all around, huddled closely together,
the square forms a lopsided rectangle. It is afternoon, a sunny day, music and noises in the
distance as if from a fair. Kaspar, passing us,
steps into the center of the square led on by the
Unknown Man. We observe both of them from
behind. In the middle of the square, the Unknown Man stops short. He looks hastily to all
sides, speaks urgently to Kaspar, who gives the
impression of total exhaustion, and then presses
a letter into Kaspar's hands. He adjusts the hand
in such a way that Kasper holds the letter out a

little, as if he were about to hand it to someone. The Unknown Man takes a step to the side, and Kaspar stands alone, swaying, clumsily holding the letter before him, into the Void. Finally, the Unknown Man takes his felt hat with the broad rim and puts it into Kaspar's other hand. Kaspar stands motionless, decorated like some sort of fowl. We realize that the Unknown Man has black hair. He leaves hastily at an angle to the side, his cape flapping all around him.

Kaspar's voice: . . .After that I must have rested twenty times, untill we came into the Big Village. When we were in the town, how ever, he hath given me a letter in to my hands and hath sayed, I must stay there, untill somebody comes and leads you there. And that I should like to be such a one rider as Father hath been. There I stayed standing for a long while, and suddenly, I saw all those houses, but then I knew not, what they were, I knew not what houses are. There in town, I came in to the World, I was borne there.

Kaspar, close. He sways slightly, trying in his clumsiness not to change his posture if possible. Over-exerted, he holds the letter outstretched into the Void and keeps his hat extended, polite and immobile in the other hand. His legs are placed one slightly before the other as if he were stopping in midstep towards someone who is not there. The toes point slightly inward, for only in this way can Kaspar strain to keep himself upright. He stands half-sunken into himself. Nothing happens. Kaspar is surprised beyond all limits. A dog crosses the empty square. Kaspar does not dare move, stretching forth his letter. Then an old man appears in the background and slouches into a house. "Orse, orse," and "Remember this," says Kaspar, maintaining his horrible posture. A little girl carrying an even smaller girl passes by. "You there," says the girl, "did you see where Annelies has gone?" Kaspar's face brightens, his lame arm with the letter is visibly gaining force. "Be rider", says Kaspar, pleased.

Some time passes again, and Kaspar still stands on the square with his hat drawn and the letter stretched out before him. The shoemaker Weickmann is leaning from the open window above his shop with his wife, a few of their green potted plants in front of them. Weickmann sucks on his cold pipe and spits some dark juice into a pot of geraniums. His fingers are brown with tobacco. We notice that he is measuring Kaspar with his gaze. His wife is staring down fixedly at that peculiar figure as well. There they lean, waiting calmly to behold whatever will happen next.

Kaspar, close. Unable to extend his arm properly any more, and lowering the letter somewhat, he nevertheless strains excessively to offer it to an imaginary recipient. His mouth is contorted by soundless weeping.

Weickmann knocks his pipe clean on his bootheel and then approaches Kaspar from the side, "What are you doing here?" says Weickmann. "As Father hath been," says Kaspar. Weickmann wants to know where he is going, whether or not he is a stranger in town, and whether he, Weickmann, can help him with the letter. "I wanto be such a one rider as Father hath been," says Kaspar. Weickmann is flabbergasted, he scans the letter more closely. "To his Excellency, Cavalry Captain of the 4th Battalion of the 6th Schwolian Reigment, N.," he reads. That is very close by, just past Augustiner Lane, the Calvalry Captain has his house right on the corner, I can show you the way there, or perhaps the young man has something else to do. Kaspar strains to explain something, but merely extirpates unintelligible sounds from within. "Orse," he says at last. Weickmann wants to know know where this fellow who seems so uncanny has come from — from Erlangen or Ansbach, or from Regensburg? "Regensburg," Kaspar repeats after him. "Ah, Regensburg," says Weickmann, pleased. "Regensburg," says Kaspar once again.

House of the Cavalry Captain

Weickmann rings the doorbell. Half-conscious, Kaspar leans against the wall beside him. Weickmann is holding the letter now. After a second more insistent ringing of the bell, a servant opens up while morosely buttoning his shirt, apparently having been roused from his slumber. This young man here has come from Regensburg, the cobbler explains, he is carrying a letter for the Captain. The Captain is not home, the servant says, and just as he is about to close the

112

door he catches himself, for this affair has struck him as being peculiar. The young man came from Regensburg, but he has not explained himself very clearly because he seems to be quite exhausted, says Weickmann; he proceeds to gesture discreetly towards the servant with his hand on his head indicating that the stranger is not in his right mind. For awhile they deliberate. The servant thinks the young man can relax a bit on the straw in the stable, as the Captain surely won't be back until nightfall, at which time the young man could deliver his letter. "Orse," says Kaspar. "Yes, in the stable with the horses, on the straw," says the servant.

Horse stable

Kaspar lies on the straw in deathlike slumber. Even while sleeping, he holds onto his hat in the way he received it. A horse bends over him gently, gazing upon him intelligently for a long time.

Weickmann has gathered the Captain, the servant, a police notary, two maids, and the shoemaker in the stable. In the background, the head of a stable boy peeks out from the hayloft. The Captain and the police notary are visibly conscious of the significance of this affair. Squinting, the Captain holds the letter out in front of him and reads:

113

Captain:"From the Bavarian border, whose place is unamed 1828. Your Excelency Sir Captain!"

Police Notary: "Excelency, ha-ha!"

Captain: "I diliver you a boy, who wants to serve his King faithfully he demands, this boy has been put to me, 1812 the 7 of October, and I myself a poor day labourer, I have 10 children also, I have enough to do myself to make ends meet, and his mother has put the child only for his education, but I could not ask for his mother, now I did not say anything that the boy has been put to me, at the Provincial Court. I have thoght to myself I should have him for my son, I have educated him Christian and from time 1812 I have not let him one step from the house, that Nobody knowed where he has been grown up, and he himself knows not how my house is called, and he doth not know the Place either, you may ask him, but he sayeth nothing. I've teached him how to read and writ, and when we ask him waht he be, he sayeth he also wants to be such a one rider, what his Father hath been. If he had parents, as he hath not, he had been a learnet fellow. You may show him anything and he knows it right awai.

Dear Mister Cavalry Captain, you must not plague him at al, he knoweth my abode not, where I stay, I have led him awai by night, he knoweth not how to go hoam. I recommend myself obedientli. I make not known my name, for I could be punisht.

And he hath no penny money with him,
becos I have nothing myself, if you keep him
not, you have to cut him off or hang him in
the chimny.''

The servant tries to wake Kaspar, the people surrounding him muse that he sleeps like a dead
man. At last they put him on his feet, but he
continues to sleep standing upright as if deeply
unconscious. Weickmann attempts to prevent the
Captain from using brute force, and explains that
the young man obviously is not too clear in his
mind, plus he can't even walk properly, rambling
more than walking.

The Captain shakes Kaspar so hard that the
horses are frightened. Kaspar opens his eyes a slit
and glances about for a moment, ready to sink
back into the recesses of his deep sleep. After a
hefty boot from the Captain's foot, Kaspar at
last comes alive, gazing into the circle, carefully
looking at their hands, however, instead of their
faces. Then he suddenly discovers the shining
brass buttons on the Captain's uniform and
nestles against them gleefully. Enthusiastically he
grabs the epaulets of the Captain who reacts
quite indignantly to this. The police notary wants
to know what his name is, where he comes from
and what his rank is. Since Kaspar simply utters
a low sound without answering, the notary asks
the same thing once more, speaking up now
doubly loud. Finally he starts to urge Kaspar in a
piercing voice. Where does he come from, who
has brought him, where is his passport, and what
is his profession! ''Rider be,'' blurts Kaspar.

This fellow's mental development seems to be in

a condition of veritable neglect, the Cavalry Captain remarks, an official interrogation conducted by the police is useless in a case such as this.

Surely he must be hungry, a maid says in the hesitant lull while handing Kaspar a slice of meat and a glass of beer. Kaspar tries some of this, but as soon as he has touched the first morsel with his mouth, his face twitching, visibly appalled and disgusted, he spits the food out. The onlookers are at a loss. Kaspar begins to moan softly and points to his feet. As the maid removes his boots they have to support him or he cannot keep himself upright on one leg; crowding in on him, the surrounding people become aware that Kaspar's feet are covered all over with blisters, most of them open and bloody. His feet are as soft as silk, says the maid. And the toenails are as soft and puffed up like bread crusts.

In accordance with the Captain's command, Kaspar's jacket is taken off and his shirt opened. The servant discovers a vaccination mark on his arm. That is a definite sign that this foundling belongs to the upper class, for they alone have their children vaccinated. He shall prepare a report on the physical condition of the foundling, for how else can the authorities determine whether or not this fellow is just some wicked impostor. Where does the wound on his elbow come from, he questions louder and louder until at last he just shouts at Kaspar.

Kaspar's jacket, closer. The servant searches his pockets, producing some printed pamphlets, and spreads them all out as the Captain dictates to the notary for the record:

Cavalry Captain: "A prayer book entitled 'Spiritual Forget-Me-Nots', a selection of beautiful and zealous matins by a devout soul, Altoettingen."

"A little rosary made of tortoise shell, with a metal crucifix."

"A German key."

"A printed brochure entitled 'Six Pious and Forceful Prayers'."

"Likewise, one entitled 'Spiritual Sentry', printed in Prague."

"A square piece of folded paper where, yes, indeed, we find a small amount of gold dust."

The boots, trousers, jacket and hat will be subjected to another, closer inspection, says the police notary. As things stand now, this forsaken looking fellow shall be detained by the authorities, he adds, to the visible relief of the Captain. There is no other possibility, for where else shall we put someone like this.

Kaspar suddenly catches sight of the police official's pencil and snatches it. They let him. Kaspar starts scribbling on the sheet of paper upon which the report has been written, first repeating single syllables as in writing exercises, then, almost illegibly: Kaspar Hauser. With everyone shouting at him at once, Kaspar shrinks completely back into himself. Apathetic and profoundly indifferent, he lets them do what they want.

Prison in the tower, the drunk tank, seen from without.

From outside: The door slams shut and Hiltel, the gray and haggard prison guard, pushes several bolts. Then he opens the little window in the door, watching the room. Through the window we see Kaspar in a corner cowering on a straw mattress, totally absentminded, barefoot and the hat still in his hands as he had received it. In deep concentration he sniffs the straw and touches it with his tongue.

Outside at the little window, the police notary, the Cavalry Captain and the servant are huddling close, seemingly visibly satisfied with this solution. Perhaps he wasn't all that unruly after all, perhaps he was even fairly good-natured, the police notary suggests. He had come with them quite willingly and did not give the impression that he wanted to make trouble for the time being, until the authorities had arranged the case well enough to take it up. They would question him under oath, for he didn't convey the image of a cretin or a madman, and would keep him for awhile in this tower for police convicts and vagabonds.

Drunk Tank, interior

The cell is fairly large, it is filled with six cots, each covered with a straw mattress and a blanket normally used to cover horses. A drunkard is lying on one of the mattresses with his back to the wall, snoring. He is thoroughly besmirched and neglected, and lies on the cot fully dressed, his shoes resting on the blanket. His shirt sticks out of his pants in the back, and the pants have slipped down almost to his tailbone; his back is covered with dirty hair. Heavy, gruesome snoring.

In front of the cot, half-dried up vomit; we can tell it was a noodle dish.

Kaspar, up close. He is completely withdrawn, in utter indifference, paying no heed to his surroundings. After lengthy brooding cowering, he revives, glancing about without comprehending anything. Then his gaze fixes upon the window, which is but lightly barred. Kaspar stumbles clumsily towards it and slowly works his way up, placing his feet down flatly and lifting his knees far too high. With his full front torso he leans against the window, still clutching the hat with his right hand. He scans the exterior with a stolid gaze but he doesn't seem to perceive anything. His eyes are a bit watery and inflamed, light floods inward over him. He has not yet come to grips with the brightness outside.

View from the window. A tower window, we are overlooking the roofs and gables of the town. Dead smoke oppresses the roofs. Two jackdaws fly past. Longer view from the window. The drunkard snores horribly and against all rules.

Drunk tank

The drunkard lies calmly, he has pulled his blanket up completely and is breathing as softly as if he were dead.

Kaspar is sitting on the floor, shoving a wooden horse back and forth as if entranced. He lets the wheels roll very quietly. Towards the entrance of the room we now behold a silent wall of people staring at Kaspar. From the entrance we feel pushing and pressing.

Kaspar glances up unperturbed, rolling his little horse on and on. He is infinitely removed and peers through the people at a still-farther profundity as if they were made of glass. Suddenly, rolling on with the horse, Kaspar utters the scream of an animal. Dreamlike, he screams.

Hiltel's apartment, the kitchen

Lunch around the kitchen table. The table has been set and Mrs. Hiltel, a mild youngish

120

woman, has taken her seat. She has placed beside her the cradle with her baby who cries every now and then. At such moments she touches the edge of the cradle with her right hand without looking, while with her left she goes on eating, undisturbed. Further back the stove crackles as a pot steams away. We realize at first glance that the furnishings are rather meager.

On the far side of the table there is a bench winding round the corner, and Hiltel and his five year-old son Julius are taking great pains there to make Kaspar sit down. He tries to slide down to the floor so he can sit with outstretched legs, and we realize instantly that Kaspar has never before eaten properly. Kaspar is newly dressed.

Hiltel lifts Kaspar unto the bench and tries to get Kaspar's legs to bend beneath the table. But in this position he topples forward onto the table. At last, after lengthy efforts with this uncouth foundling, Hiltel puts Kaspar at the corner of the table, permitting him to stretch out his legs on the bench alongside the table. Julius hands Kaspar a cup of water and the latter grabs it like his jug with both hands, hastily emptying it with a single draught. He holds the empty cup for such a long time that Julius eventually takes it from him. Julius grows into the role of teacher with considerable ease and obviously enjoys instructing someone so much older than himself. He shows Kaspar, by guiding his hand into the cup that the cup is empty. The he turns the cup upside down and the last drop drips slowly onto the table. Holding the cup, he shows it to Kaspar and repeats: empty. Kaspar also says "empty", although he probably hasn't grasped it yet. He apparently thinks "cup", since he grabs another cup which is still full while saying "empty".

"I say," says Hiltel proudly, "that chap isn't so bad, he is proving himself to be quite nimble. He is merely lacking manners."

Julius puts a spoon into Kaspar's hand and pushes forth a bowl of soup. In a pronounced manner he mimicks the way to handle it. Kaspar tries this as well, but at first he doesn't touch his mouth with the strange instrument. When he finally manages to try the soup, he shudders with disgust and refuses to take anything else but bread.

One would have to get him accustomed to normal food quite gradually, Hiltel remarks to his wife, one would have to summon a great deal of patience to turn this half-ferocious beast-man into a decent chap.

Prison in the tower, drunk tank

The drunkard, who in the interim has sobered up, is sitting twisted up on a cot. He is pressing his bent arms into his body and softly moaning. He has a coarse face distorted by the booze, and one of his ears is squashed like a sprout. "Jesus Maria," says the man, "my guts are killing me." Beside him is an old rancid tramp, a newcomer raising hell in his delirium. He curses and roars,

"Fire, it's burning." Kaspar's corner. He sits in his customary position on the floor beside Julius, serious like an adult. Julius pinches Kaspar's index finger. "Finger," says Kaspar. He taps Kaspar's hand. "Arm," says Kaspar. "No, hand," says Julius, "the arm is the whole part up to here." "Hand," Kaspar corrects himself, and then runs his right hand all along his left arm up to his shoulder and says "Arm." He is happy, he has understood.

"Fire, fire, the tower's burning," screams the old man in his corner.

But Kaspar and Julius are so preoccupied that they don't hear him. Julius touches Kaspar's mouth. "Mouth," says Kaspar forthwith, and then "nose", tapping his own nose simultaneously. "And this is the ear," says Julius, touching Kaspar's ear. "Ear," says Kaspar while touching his head with a frightened gesture. He fondles his ear excitedly, it obviously is a sensational discovery for him. "Yes, it really belongs to you, that you can truly believe," says Julius. "And there you have another one," and pinches his other one. Kaspar looks incredulous and confused. Then Julius pulls the ear very hard, and Kaspar begins to realize that this ear really belongs to him. "Fire-ho," screams the old man, and "Waitress, bring me a beer!"

Julius takes a small round mirror from his pocket and holds it in front of Kaspar's face. There, that is really your ear. Kaspar backs off, frightened, and when Julius brings the mirror even closer, Kaspar lowers his eyes evading the mirror like an animal. Julius won't give up, he pulls Kaspar's ear and several times says "ear" quite loudly. Kaspar finally gets up his courage and looks; his gaze is that of a hare. He has yet to comprehend that he is seeing himself. Bewildered, he leans forward to search behind the mirror. "Waitress," the one in the corner cries, "I have to pee."

Wash House, the First Bath

Kaspar sits in a big washtub with Julius who is obviously there to rid him of his fear of water. The water steams slightly from the heat. Kaspar has the flesh of a larva. The prison guard's wife adds some more water because it is still too hot. Kaspar, feeling fine and uttering sounds of well-being starts kicking and splashing about in the water just like a small child. Julius blows a small paper boat across towards Kaspar's chest, and he pats it gleefully with the palm of his hand. The woman starts to soap Kaspar down, poking into his ears with a rag to his displeasure. Then she stands him upright in the tub to soap down the lower part of his body; Kaspar permits this without self-conciousness and is unperturbed. He stands there like a horse. Frau Hiltel constantly tries to excuse herself, though this is completely unnecessary, by soothing Kaspar and telling him that he must not be ashamed before her, since only God is looking on.

All at once Kaspar perceives how a solid year-old layer of dirt is peeling off him and how his transluscent white skin begins to emerge underneath. Fine little veins shimmer through from within. He turns to the woman fearfull. "Mother," says Kaspar, "the skin!"

Prison in the tower, feigned fencing

Kaspar sits slumped into himself in the drunk tank as a peculiar scene takes place. He is on the floor with his legs outstretched in front of him playing with his toy horses, oblivious to his surroundings. The two companions have gone. Kaspar's mattress has been stuffed with fresh straw, and on a new shelf are a dozen or so wooden animals on wheels neatly arranged in a row.

Before Kaspar stands a uniformed cavalry lieutenant who is sticking and striking at Kaspar with his drawn sword, although not really touching him. He pauses momentarily and then lunges forth with a loud "Ha!" and makes a wild thrust past Kaspar's skull. Next he attempts to feign in the French manner with graceful dancing steps, finally fidgeting with his sword in front of Kaspar's face. Kaspar is utterly absorbed in his playing and glances up only once, abstractedly, looking through the sword beyond. The cocky

Lieutenant now aims a cruel swishing blow blindly in the air. He stops, astonished but visibly proud of his extraordinary prowess, and then turns around.

Only now do we realize that there are about ten more people in the room who have quietly witnessed this spectacle while pressed against the wall near the entrance. They begin whispering amongst themselves, and a police officer remarks that he no longer thinks that this fellow is a cruel impostor since he obviously has no feeling or concept of danger. He hasn't been frightened at all. The Lieutenant makes one last impressive parry.

The Lieutenant approaches Kaspar with a burning candle. Kaspar looks up and makes pleasurable sounds as he fondles the shiny brass buttons of the uniformed Lieutenant's jacket. Now Kaspar notices the candle standing close to him on the floor. He grabs rapturously at the flame but plucks and twists the wick with his fingers much too long. He jerks his hand back and, his mouth grimacing hideously, he starts to cry. He cries without a sound.

Hiltel's apartment

Very tender scene. As Kaspar is half-bent over the suckling's cradle we see that he doesn't really dare move further, there is some sort of taboo hovering in the air. Kaspar has put his right hand into the cradle and is trying to withdraw it again carefully.

We now see the infant closely. He is barely six months old and has an embroidered bonnet on his head. He grips Kaspar's index fingers tightly with one of his hands and won't let go. Kaspar cautiously bends his finger and the little one in the cradle laughs.

Kaspar suddenly senses that someone is watching from behind; he bends forward very carefully and gently tries to pull his finger away, but the baby won't let go. Kaspar doesn't dare pull any harder.

We see Frau Hiltel, the mother of the suckling, standing in the doorway, watching Kaspar quietly and trying to make up her mind.

Kaspar slowly turns around and, with an expression of guilt-ridden despair in his face, he looks into the woman's face. He wants to free himself from the cradle but is unable to do so, as we can see how he lifts up the tiny hand of the infant over the cradle's edge with his own.

The woman smiles at Kaspar and prompts herself inwardly. She instinctively does the right thing: she takes the little one out of the cradle and decisively places him in Kaspar's arms. The latter is frightened with emotion. He delicately sniffs at the little one's head, fondling him ever so gently, more like a blind man than one who sees. "Mother," Kaspar strains to speak, his mouth twisted amid the tears, "everything is removed from me."

Four farmboys have broken into the cell, and one can realize instantly that they're up to no good. They are standing around trying to look innocent. Kaspar sits on the floor with a picture of a plum before him that he is attempting to copy. "I am honored," says Kaspar to his visitors contentedly, happy because he has said it right. While sitting on the floor he bows, and his ears turn red. The squinting boys don't look him straight in the eye.

The one with coarse features hiding behind the others carefully places a chicken on the floor in back of the others. And what a chicken! It is a huge black puffed-up hen with an incredibly stupid face, and the boys have adorned her breast with a medal which hangs from wide ribbon around its neck. When the fellow to the rear pushes the hen towards Kaspar through the legs of one of his friends — a flap-eared yokel who stands there expectantly — we instantly become aware of something else: the chicken is utterly drunk.

One of the fellows says "hmmm!" while putting yet another piece of bread dipped in schnapps into his mouth. The he stumbles forward, turns around and doubles back. Blathering nonsensically it heads straight for Kaspar and, trying to peck at the medal, it falls flat on its face. When the chicken finally manages to struggle onto its legs again, Kaspar notices it.

Kaspar stands up with a start. "Black," says

Kaspar frightfully, "black, black." The chicken now screeches with delight, puts its head on the floor and does a somersault. Full of dread and trembling horribly, Kaspar clings to his pillow and retreats to the farthest corner of the room. He tries scrambling up the wall for refuge near the ceiling.

The four of them jeer and heckle crudely now, passing around their bottle while they pick up the hen and, guffawing, leave.

Prison in the tower, drunk tank

Kaspar sits on the floor surrounded by dried herbs and pressed flowers which he has neatly arranged on white sheets of paper. On his shelf is a crazy collection of wooden horses on wheels, each is precisely positioned acording to height.

In front of Kaspar stands a cute little girl about four years old, quite lively and burning with fervor, she is obviously a friend of the five year-old Julius who, as little as he is, radiates a kind of paternal dignity.

"Good morning, white kitten," says Kaspar, pressing the thumb and index finger of his right hand into an odd circle while spreading out the other three fingers in the air. He beats the rhythm of his words on the floor with his peculiarly-positioned fingers.

"You've lost your mitten," says the girl.

"You've lost, you've lost," says Kaspar, all of this moving much too fast for him.

The girl assumes the serious demeanor of a school teacher and recites the rhyme with her best behavior:

Good morning white kitten,
You've lost your mitten,
And is that milk yours or mine?
I'll lap here,
You lap there,
Lap, lap, lap this milk so fine,
Lap, lap, lap as good as wine!

The rhyme makes a profound impression upon Kaspar who listens to the girl with bulging eyes. Then, for the very first time, a great heartful laughter shines forth from his face. Kaspar exults and utters jubilant cries. The girl is proud in a very ladylike manner, bobbing a little curtsy.

"Agnes," says Julius after a while, "that was still too long, he doesn't understand yet."

Prison in the tower, drunk tank, evening

"Two pints you drink, and two pints you pee," Kaspar says obediently. Some depraved-looking youngsters cluster around him, encouraging him to say it more distinctly. They can hardly contain their laughter. Cheap beastly thrills. Kaspar, unsuspecting, is learning zealously.

Prison in the tower, drunk tank, exterior

Several prominent people are jostling outside the little grated window, pushing for a peep inside. From within we hear disgruntled sounds and Julius' jolly laughter.

The mayor whispers to the prefect of police that the foundling was once a member of a troop of English equestrians, but had deserted while they were stationed in the Upper Palatinate. This was questionable, however. But he was quite sure that the rampant rumors linking him to the Royal House of Baden, alleging that he was banished from the line of succession to the throne, are totally false, since if this were the case they would have disposed of him altogether. Furthermore, the House of Baden is above suspicion, even if its line of succession was rather controversial. He could not believe all of that anyway because the fellow had somewhat coarse and indelicate features, displaying none of the natural nobility that is found in those of royal blood. One also must begin to consider just how the fellow could commence paying his own way, since for the moment he was living on the public trust. Someone had to think of a way he could contribute to his own upkeep, perhaps by taking advantage of the public interest in him.

Again he turns to the little window to watch, half amused and half disgusted at what was taking place inside the cell.

Drunk tank, interior

Only Kaspar's cot remains in the room, over in the corner, the others have been removed but for the impressions from their legs that we can clearly see left on the floor. Kaspar sits with his knees extended on the floor, holding a cat between his widespread legs that is forever trying to escape. "With the hands with the hands," says Kaspar to the cat as he tries to teach her how to eat with her paws and lift the food neatly up to her mouth. Julius, sitting next to him, is bursting with laughter. Kaspar is quite serious about his task and refuses to be disturbed by the cat's wiggling and twisting.

He finally attempts with utter gravity to teach the cat how to walk upright. He places her on her hind legs, and the cat hisses angrily and suddenly claws him on his hands. Terribly bewildered and totally horrified, Kaspar lets the animal go. He gets no help from Julius, who is laughing even harder now.

Kaspar, deeply disturbed, grabs his wool and his knitting and withdraws into himself, beginning to knit with his fat clumsy fingers. He has already finished a piece as big as the palm of his hand. We have no idea where it came from.

Tent at the Fair, interior, Four Riddles of the Universe

The fair is shabby, the tent dilapidated, the festivities awash in a profound sadness. The atmosphere is filled with gloom, which is all the more striking since the visitors do not notice it in their desire to amuse themselves. Many people are pressing inward, the tent is almost full. There are a lot of women and children, even drunkards as well, who behave in a particularly raucous manner.

We can see a bit of light shimmering through a shabby transparent curtain that has been in a semi-circle. There is some movement behind the curtain, then it freezes into a rigid stillness as the director steps onto the tiny stage from the side. Dressed in circus garb with lots of glitter and shiny black patent-leather boots, he wields a wooden pointer in his hand.

He bids the audience welcome. "Ladies and Gentlemen!" he shouts to quiet down the troublemakers, as he wishes to present to the public The Four Riddles of the Universe, all together in a single place for the very first time. He begs the adults to keep their children at a safe distance for piety permits no childish pranks. They can step up a bit, but only as far as this line here. Music from a merry-go-round outside is drowning out his words. He raises his voice to introduce the first Riddle, The Little King. Behind the curtain a fanfare blares forth.

He gives a wink and with several jerks the curtain opens, but only wide enough to see The Little King.

A throne has been placed on a slightly-elevated wooden platform, a huge ample throne richly decorated with carvings and golden glitter. The Little King cowers in a corner of the throne as if exiled. The Little King is a tiny midget about forty years old with an old man's wrinkled face. His skin is shriveled like a leathery apple. He wears little white boots with a small ermine coat made of rabbit's fur around his shoulders. Holding both arms outstretched, he barely manages to reach the armrests of the throne with his fingertips. A large, impressive crown is hanging from a rope above his head. Two poodles in gold embroidered uniforms stand at attention on their hind legs before him. The Little King seems apathetic as he contemplates the crowd.

This is the King of Punt, the legendary land of gold, the director exclaims, he descends from an ancient race of giants. But, in the course of time, one king after the other became smaller than his predecessor, and as of now this was the last one of the line. If the lineage were to continue for a couple of centuries more, one would not be able to see the last King of Punt for he would skip away like a flea.

Tremendous curiosity amongst the greatly enraptured public, particularly amongst the children.

Now, if the people in front would kindly move on and make room for those behind them who also want to have a look, next comes Mozart. The curtain opens a little wider. Behind it sits a gentle boy about seven years old with the face of a prince. He is dressed like a little gentleman in a rococco costume, holding a piece of drainpipe made of paper-mache in front of him. It is painted black inside, he stares into it incessantly.

The director shouts out that Mozart didn't start to talk until the age of three, but once he did, he asked for nothing but the music of Mozart. Night and day he longed obsessively for Mozart. By the time he was five he knew all the scores by heart. Now he doesn't talk any more, as he is only interested in dark holes in the ground, in cave entrances and drainage ditches that capture his attention and enable him to meditate upon the blackness within. He stopped speaking altogether at the age of five when they tried to teach him how to read and write at school. He couldn't do it, he said, because the bright whiteness of the paper blinded him. Since then he has refused to speak.

The audience is already pushing onward, and with a new fanfare the curtain opens further. The director cries out that next will be a live tribal show, with an Indian savage from the New Spanish Realm of the Sun.

The Indian, Hombrecito appears from behind the curtain, a lean feeble-minded man with an enchanted look. He is wearing three coats, one on top of the other, and across his shoulders he carries a folded embroidered Indian poncho. He wears a beautiful Indian woolen cap with ear flaps and reddish embroidery on his nearly clean-shaven skull. His pants come down to just past the knees so his calves are naked like exposed cables, and on his feet he is wearing sandals. As soon as the curtain opens, he starts to play a strange beautiful melody on some sort of Indian panpipe made of bound bamboo stems. The children in particular push to get close to him.

The director tells the audience that this savage is the only living member of the original Native and Indian Show that once toured Europe. He plays his flute because he believes that if he stopped, the townspeople would die. He always wears three coats at once to protect himself from colds and, as he says, against the breath of people. He is quite a jovial fellow and very well-behaved, but he doesn't speak a word of any language other than his Indian dialect.

And now, the greatest of The Four Riddles, the director proclaims, and as the curtain opens completely amid the fanfare, there is Kaspar, The Foundling. He explains that Kaspar has expressed his willingness to appear here every afternoon with the consent of the authorities, in order to ease his financial burden on the community.

We see Kaspar on a dais and realize instantly that he doesn't have the slightest idea what this is all about, that he doesn't even understand how he got here. Kaspar is standing on his own wooden platform, with a thick ornamental rope stretched between four posts so no one can get too close to him. Kaspar stands there the same way he was found in N., dressed the same, in the same tortured posture with one foot a little in front of the other, the letter in his left hand extended towards an imaginary recipient, and his hat in his right hand, politely removed.

The people crowd in more closely, curious but

rather shy. The director talks while pointing with his stick, explaining about Kaspar, going on and on. No longer can we comprehend what he says because music is setting in, strong and solemn. Long shot. Kaspar is beset by the same dreamlost, gruesome and forlorn confusion as on the Tallow Square the day he was born in the town of N.

We see Daumer standing amongst the spectators in the background. He seems to be the only one there who understands.

Behind the circus tent

Kaspar and Hombrecito are sitting behind the tent in front of a cage on wheels with somewhat narrow but very strong wooden bars. Julius runs by one time in the background with a stick and a hoop. The backs of some primitive stalls and tents all around. Grass trodden under foot, straw trampled into the clay. A small dung heap and pitchforks, everything is rather bleak. Hombrecito patiently plays his flute to himself, playing for the bear.

The cage, close. Inside we can recognize the figure of a bear, lying apathetically on the dirty straw on the floor of the cage. He wears a heavy leather muzzle over his snout which he pokes between the bars a bit. The bear breathes deeply and exhaustedly, steadily gazing upon the two visitors outside.

"The bear is sick," says Kaspar, practicing the sentence. "The bear is sick, the bear is sick," he says, learning the sentence that he has obviously just picked up from Julius. With an other-wordly expression, Hombrecito plays. They eye each other for a very long time.

Open field, the grandfather, father and son

Far away in the distance we see an excited crowd running across the field, a charming landscape with half-grown fields of wheat that are still green. A pronounced clamor. And now we notice that even further away three figures are running, far in front of the others. Somewhat closer, the three fugitives. Mozart, Hombrecito and Kaspar have escaped, they are racing across the fields. Flat-footed, Kaspar runs with long awkward bounds. Hombrecito with his skinny calves is in the lead, he has unbuttoned all three coats, and bringing up the rear is Mozart, who is hampered by his rococco costume. He is the first one to get stuck when their escape route takes them over a small canal. Right there is a drainpipe that runs into the ground, black and mysterious. Mozart suddenly stops and, squatting down, stares into the black opening wondrously. He lapses at once into a profound trance.
The pursuers, including the director, the police notary, and Daumer spread out a little; a few of them stay with Mozart to take care of him, others

continue the chase and visibly gain ground. There are approximately a dozen people, several women amongst them as well.

Kaspar slows down and Hombrecito moves ahead ever further, though realizing that the pursuers are faster than he. In a small lovely hollow, three maple trees appear in a row: a tall one, a medium-sized one, and finally a young one whose trunk is still thin. They look like grandfather, father and son, and from the shouts of the pursuers, we clearly learn that these are really their names. Close by, on the forest fringe, is an apiary, with a dense grove of spruce saplings behind it. Hombrecito flees up into the son, in his confusion he has seized upon the thinnest tree and it can hardly support him.

Kaspar, having taken the lead, reaches the edge of the woods. He disappears amongst the spruces and we last see him changing directions. "Stop," the police notary shrieks after Kaspar, "stay where you are, I say," he gasps, stopping short himself.

About half of the group storms forward into the spruce grove and search about in it, as we can see by the trembling of the little trees which are a little taller than the average man. They yell for Kaspar and wonder what is the matter with him, whether or not he has lost his mind.

Hombrecito, meanwhile, has climbed so high into the Son that if he goes any higher, the entire trunk will bend over. Therefore no one dares to follow him up the tree.

He should come down, bellows the notary, who considers himself the leader because he has a uniform on. He will ruin the tree which had been planted but three years ago by Heuser's grandson. Why doesn't he pick the Father or Grandfather for his ridiculous escapades? Hombrecito does not answer, gazing down calmly at his pursuers. What does he want, the director calls up to him, he makes a good living, he has nothing to complain about. Finally, one of the men climbs up the thin trunk after Hombrecito. The whole trunk slowly bends over, and Hombrecito is plucked from the branches like a piece of fruit.

One after the other the pursuers reappear at the edge of the spruce grove. He couldn't have simply disappeared, one of them says. They will have to search this part of the forest again, but this time more systematically, not so haphazardly. He couldn't be any place else but in there.

Daumer stands quietly at the edge of the forest, thinking hard. He then walks decisively around the apiary and opens a little tool shed. There, amongst the boards, tools and honeycomb frames cowers Kaspar apathetically, his face glowing like red-hot iron, as it was at the outset in the cellar. He notices no one and nothing, taking no heed of Daumer, still sitting quietly.

View over the fields. The people stand together peacefully beneath a cluster of trees. A solemn music ensues.

Kaspar at the window, winter's day

Kaspar is standing at the window gazing out
silently over the garden. It is winter outside, time
passes. The bottom part of the pane is frozen
over. Nothing stirs; someone is leaning over the
rail of the footbridge at the far end of the garden, staring motionlessly at the frozen creek. A
raven stands still in the snow-covered garden
cawing hoarsely, his breath visibly frozen. Then,
tottering, he walks away directly into the Imaginary. Kaspar sniffs quietly.
A grandfather clock chimes somewhere in the
house below.

Daumer's room, interior

Almost at ground level, it is a spacious room
with imposing windows. It is summer, and the
song of a solitary bird is heard from outside;
through an open window we see black currant
bushes and part of the garden. The walnut tree
outside rustles softly. The room is furnished
pragmatically, with pictures hanging on the wall
and shelves filled with books which are stacked
so disorderly that you instantly know these books
are really being read.
Kaspar sits at the piano in the foreground. He
now sports a downy moustache on his upper lip,

making it apparent that much time has passed. But something else is evident also: Kaspar still betrays a neglected air about him. His movements are still bizarre, and though he isn't ill-groomed, he gives the impression of needing a bath badly. His countenance bears a certain crude melancholy.

Kaspar is a dilettante at the piano, playing the simple "Virgin Chorus" from "Der Frei-schuetz". He frequently hits the wrong key and with every false note gesticulates wildly with his hands. His movements seem jerky, eccentric, and as yet unassured. Daumer stands behind Kaspar wearing a frock coat, listening contentedly to his ward's playing. Daumer seems learned, paternal, with lively eyes and an unhealthy pale complexion. His posture is slightly stooped. We notice that the few times he corrects Kaspar, he does so affectionately.

Kaspar suddenly stops and turns towards Daumer. He cannot continue, he cannot concentrate, "it" feels so strong inside his breast.

Kaspar moves to the window and gazes out into the garden. Daumer follows him, paternally placing a hand on his shoulder without saying a word. He, says Kaspar, he feels so "unexpectedly" old. Prolonged silence; Daumer doesn't say anything, because he apparently feels it is not good to say anything.

Walk through the garden

The garden is rather large, not too tidy, with
idyllic nooks that are somewhat neglected, more
or less like an English garden. There are also
some huge walnut trees, a pergola covered with
clusters of lilacs, black currant bushes, gooseber-
ries, plus a few flower and vegetable beds; a
halfway practical garden. At the edge of the
garden is a dense hedge of small beeches which
hasn't been trimmed for quite some time. Beyond
it, off to the side, a slender canal with a railed
footbridge. A poorly-raked gravel path runs
around the garden, overgrown with weeds. A little bench and a garden table sit under the walnut
tree. The exterior of the house is tressed by a
pear tree which covers nearly the entire front wall
facing the garden and is supported by a trellis.
Kaspar and Daumer are rounding the garden in
pensive silence. Kaspar still lifts his knees up high
as he walks, placing the whole foot down on the
ground. Kaspar's speech continues to have a
peculiar cadence and choice of words. If he gets
stuck or is searching for a word, he confusedly
scans the vacant space in the sentence with his index finger in the air.
"It has dreamed in me," says Kaspar. You
should tell me, says Daumer. Walking silently for
a while, Kaspar gathers words instead of speaking, delicately moving his lips. After awhile
Daumer says he is pleased with Kaspar's pro-
gress, for only two weeks ago he still thought his
dreams were real, as indicated by his recollection

of a visit with the Mayor's wife, who had in fact been away on a trip for several weeks. Kaspar nods.

It was also strange that he, Kaspar, hadn't begun to dream earlier; in his first prison he hadn't dreamed at all, since he was unable to imagine anything, but afterwards — why hadn't he dreamed then? Or had he dreamed and mistaken it for reality, not recognizing the difference? After some strenuous reflection, Kaspar says he can't be sure if he was actually in his prison or a different prison, and, as for this walking, whether or not it is a dream. It had dreamed in him from the Caucasus, he had been in the Caucasus.

Yes, he had learned about that during his lessons, Daumer says, pleased; that is where the dream must stem from. But, says Kaspar, he had seen the Caucasus very distinctly. First there had been a strange village on a mountainside, with white houses and steps rather than streets, and on the steps there was water running.

Vision of the Caucasus

All at once we see what Kaspar is relating, it is mysterious and strange and flickering. We see a village on a steep incline, a very alien Southern place, with whitewashed steps converging from all sides into one main road of steps. Water is running on each of the steps, flowing into brooks.

Then, says Kaspar, stopping short in his walk, he had seen the Caucasus, towering red-colored mountains, and beyond them there was a plain filled with houses, white ones, each by itself as if from another world. These dwellings reached as far as his eye could see. He had looked "over yonder."

We behold towering mountains, gazing down from the peaks. The air and the clouds are colored deep purple from the setting sun. In the haze we discover a mountain range, then behind it another one, then further below a third, and behind that one, becoming ever more glassy and transparent, a fourth, fifth, sixth, onward into unfathomable depths. The gaze roams over these incredible mountains, the incredible purple. Then, suddenly, we see a vast plain. And in the plain there are mysterious temples with high, white, pointed towers, richly decorated like buildings from some other star. The gaze reaches far and, into the depths, as far as the gaze can wander, there is nothing but unreal structures upon this vast plain. There are hundreds of them, we are in the grip of vertigo. The images are strange and flickering, unlike anything we have ever seen before, utterly otherwordly.

Daumer's room, interior

Kaspar is sitting opposite a superior force of four pastors. On a little table there is a pot and cups of tea, but Kaspar, who is obviously feeling uncomfortable, doesn't touch his. The housekeeper Katy, a plump goodnatured country woman, brings a small platter of biscuits and withdraws immediately.

The pastors nibble primly on the proffered delicacies. Fuhrmann, with a flesh-swollen face, moss on his teeth and his collar still stained with egg yolk from breakfast, sits beside Kaspar, who evades the man's breath by necessity. As he speaks one sees his bad teeth; the other three present themselves a bit less obtrusively.

Fuhrmann wants to know if Kaspar had a natural conception of God while imprisoned, looking over at his colleagues pregnantly.

Kaspar speaks strenuously, knocking each beat with his hand. He doesn't understand this question, he only knows that he hadn't thought of anything in prison. He doesn't understand at all what they had told him some time ago. He cannot imagine how God created everything out of nothing, as he was lacking the concepts for that.

The clergymen put their heads together taking council amongst themselves, seeing if someone can make this comprehensible to him. He simply has to believe, says Fuhrmann, pushing a little closer to Kaspar, for to search through the darker elements of the Creed too precisely was sinful. Kaspar says that he can't understand any of this, they are talking too loudly, and he would have to learn to read and write much better to comprehend this. No, says Fuhrmann, he must learn these things above and beyond everything else. But, says Kaspar, when he, Kaspar, wants to make something, he needs something to make it with, so they should tell him how God makes something out of nothing.

He should stop, says Fuhrmann, beating his index finger on the table constantly while talking. In that case, Kaspar says, speaking will be even harder for him. This ends the discussion. A disagreeable silence spreads. The four clergymen maintain their silence towards Kaspar for a while, then they put their heads together. Finally, Fuhrmann says that Kaspar should repeat after him. He proceeds to recite a prayer. Kaspar displays an obvious reluctance in repeating it.

Narrow lane, prison tower from outside

It is just before noon; Kaspar and Daumer are standing in front of the prison tower. Kaspar gazes upward in amazement.

That is really very high, he says, it must have been a very tall man who built that. I would like to make his acquaintance. Daumer tries to explain to him that the builder had been of quite a normal height, that they had worked with scaffolds, he would take him to a construction site this very day. He wondered if Kaspar still remembered having lived in this tower.

That is hardly possible, for his room had been but a few steps long, says Kaspar. Daumer doesn't understand this contradiction at first. The house in which he had lived had to be even smaller then, not as big as the tower. Correcting Kaspar, Daumer attempts to make plain the fact that a room was always smaller than a house. This doesn't sit well with Kaspar. The room was wherever he turned, he had the room on all sides; but he could only look at the house from one side and when he turned it wasn't there any more. It didn't extend in all directions as a room would. Daumer suspends any further explanations to a later date. Kaspar doesn't seem satisfied, neither does Daumer.

Daumer's living room

Kaspar sits at his writing desk while Daumer observes from behind, looking over his shoulder at his writing. Without concentrating properly, Kaspar makes an effort to translate a simple Latin text.

He would prefer to hear something about the vast desert of the Sahara, and whether or not it was really so far away, and whether or not he might go there one day to look at it, says Kaspar. Besides, he would greatly prefer going out into the streets than translating Latin, as sitting seems very hard to him, and Latin as well.

Knowledge of the Latin tongue was indispensable for learning German, Daumer teaches him. To learn German thoroughly one had to have a thorough knowledge of Latin.

Kaspar continues working attentively for a while. Whether the Roman had to learn German thoroughly in order to read and write proper Latin, this he would like to know. Daumer ignores this question, pressing in even closer so as to remonstrate Kaspar.

Daumer's garden, gravel path

Kaspar, Daumer and Fuhrmann are gathering apples, which cover the ground where the gravel path forms a loop. Kaspar straightens up, gazing at the apple tree.

Kaspar, close. How beautiful this tree would be if its leaves were as beautifully red as the apples. Then he would be able to tolerate this tree much better. Daumer drops an apple, which rolls some distance along the gravel path. Daumer wants to pick up the apple again. It is tired now, says Kaspar, it is tired from walking; they shouldn't plague it any longer. Daumer tries to teach Kaspar that there is no life in the apple, that it was up to him which direction the apple would take, and that it would drop where he threw it. He

149

tosses an apple along the path to demontrate. But the apple skips onward after touching the ground, which provides Kaspar with opposite proof that reinforces his viewpoint.

Daumer now attempts to instruct Kaspar not so much by argument, but by continued visual demonstration. He rolls an apple along the path towards Fuhrmann, who extends his foot to stop the apple, to show that by his will the apple comes to a halt. The apple has so much momentum, however, that it jumps over the shoe and rolls on. Kaspar is exceedingly pleased by the nimbleness and intelligence of the apple, admonishing the one in his hand to do likewise before he lets it roll. The apple skips over Fuhrmann's shoe. Kaspar is jubilant, while Daumer and Fuhrmann have nothing further to say for the time being.

Kitchen in Daumer's House

Kaspar sits at the kitchen table, expertly ladling the soup in front of him with a hearty appetite. The housekeeper Katy busies herself over several pots at the stove, and slices some vegetables. The kitchen is suitably ample in size.

Why hadn't she always prepared the soup like this, he liked it now, yes, it is alright like this, says Kaspar.

Katy looks at him in amusement. Ah, says she,

the young man has never before had soup like this, heretofore feeling nothing but disgust for all dishes always, except for bread, and now he was gradually getting used to normal food. But beer and coffee still don't agree with him. Kaspar nods approvingly, resuming his eating with a good appetite.

After a pause Kaspar asks what women were made for, could Katy tell him. They really don't seem to be useful for anything more than sitting around; they are persons who don't occupy themselves with any serious work except sewing, at best, or cooking and knitting a bit. Katy stops working. He should address himself to Mr. Daumer about this, for he would have a decent answer. He had already asked him, but he didn't know anything either. Kaspar lapses into contemplation. Absorbed in his thoughts, he makes a sketch with his soup spoon on the wooden table.

Yes, says Kaspar after lengthy brooding, Mr. Daumer knows so much that he, Kaspar, would never be able to catch up with him. Mr. Daumer had told him of the desert, he couldn't get that out of his head. He wondered if she, Katy, had ever been in the desert. By no means, says Katy, she had only been in Erlangen, once. From there it was still quite a ways to the desert. Kaspar now directs the conversation further, aiming at something definite: he has invented a story about the desert and has always wanted to relate it to Mr. Daumer. Why haven't you told it to Mr. Daumer, says Katy. Yes, he doesn't know the actual story yet, only the beginning, says Kaspar, and Mr. Daumer said he wanted to hear the story as a whole, that Kaspar should think it out first before telling it. If she, Katy, would like to hear the beginning of the story, it wasn't very long.

Some other time, young man, says Katy, untying her apron strings; she would like to listen, but now she must run to the market. Kaspar is visibly disappointed. He outlines figures on the table with his spoon, breathing very softly.

Kaspar's chamber, Kaspar lonesome in his bed.

Kaspar lies in bed weeping, trying to do so quietly, he merely makes his mouth more contorted. He lies very still, until dusk. Very quiet, long scene. The half-torn curtain cannot be drawn. In front of the window outside, the leaves of the pear tree are lightly stirring.

After a while music sets in, a beautiful, calm and unstrained aria sung by a tenor. In a corner of the room the mice are rustling. We hear faraway footsteps from without.

Garden, red currant bushes

Kaspar and Daumer stand close to each other, picking red currants. They work next to one another for a long time.

It cannot be possible, says Daumer after a long pause, that for Kaspar the only agreeable thing in this world is his bed, and that everything else was ever so bad. Surely he at least loved this garden.

Kaspar doesn't answer, working his way through the bushes. Something is at work inside of him. He is strongly moved, but he doesn't find the words. It is a prolonged ponderous silence.

Yes, Kaspar says after a long pause, his appearance in this world had been a "hard fall".

Kaspar's chamber

Kaspar is sitting in his little room writing zealously with a pen. He already has filled several pages with his neat child-like handwriting. In his zeal he doesn't notice that Daumer has entered quietly.

He suddenly recoils in shock upon realizing that Daumer is standing behind him. There is no need to be frightened, Daumer says. Daumer wants to know how far along he is with the description of his life, because the news has spread and the public was waiting impatiently for his report.

Small ballroom, interior

Lively activity amongst the festive people in the brightly lit ballroom this evening: ladies in fine attire, gentlemen, noblemen, and uniformed servants taking champagne around. A light clinking of glasses, stylized amusement and polished conversation. A rumor clinks faintly about; all eyes turn to a small hallway leading into a side wing, where Lord Stanhope and Kaspar emerge.

Kaspar is very embarrassed. He doesn't want any of this to leave his hands, for he still doesn't know many words and there was so much still for him to understand, as he hasn't been in this world too long yet.

He has come, says Daumer, to inform him, Kaspar, that an English earl—His Excellency, Lord Stanhope—was residing in town, that he was taking particular interest in Kaspar's fate and was nurturing the intention of taking Kaspar to England with him as his son, if he were to make a good impression on him. This means that there would be quite a future for him. The lord has invited them to a ball he is giving tomorrow, and people of rank and reputation will be present. Tomorrow, immediately following breakfast he will accompany him to the tailor and borrow a coat for this occasion.

Kaspar is a bit confused and wants to contradict him, but he cannot think of anything except for the fact that he does not know how to dance. There is no need for that, Daumer reassures him, and withdraws once again.

154

The two of them, closer. Stanhope, about fifty, very suave and worldly in his manners, dressed like a dandy in his English outfit, with Kaspar beside him in a black frock coat and white gloves. He has removed his right glove and holds it with his left hand or rather, he clings to it. He seems to be strangled and utterly helpless. His movements resemble those of a dancing bear. When he turns to face someone, he not only turns his head but his entire body along with it.

Daumer is behind them, dressed festively as well, and two uniformed persons further beyond. Stanhope is talking German almost without an accent, and from his phraseology we gather that he is delighted with how well he can speak. He feigns intimacy with Kaspar, as if he has been his special protege for quite some time.

The earl introduces Kaspar, showing him off all around. The ladies in particular exhibit their shrill enthusiasm. Kaspar, visibly suffering, reaches forth with his right hand and makes a forced bow, then he turns his body clumsily a little further, making a bow to another lady. The ladies are enraptured by this funny little animal. The earl basks in Kaspar's presence.

How had it been in his dark prison, an elderly dame immediately wants to know. Kaspar, obviously incapable of evasions, answers: he had been happy there, he had felt quite well. The earl is a little indignant, directing the topic of conversation at once to Kaspar's remarkable progress in Latin, as well as his entire education. Daumer shows that he feels honored.

Stanhope and Kaspar increasingly become the center of attention amongst the guests, who are closing in upon the two in a circle. His young protege, the earl proclaims, was obviously the very best proof of how a noble heart cannot be spoiled or hampered in its development by even the vilest crime. Genius and Grace had now fully awakened in the young man's breast. A pure soul had come to life within him.

The surrounding people display their approval as Stanhope sinks into Rapture. Then, suddenly, something stirring in Kaspar turns to stone. He mustn't be frightened by all of these guests, he should say in all his youthful naivete whatever was moving him, Stanhope encourages him. "Your Honor," blurts Kaspar, "there is nothing more that lives inside me but my life."

Stanhope is visibly irritated.

Kaspar begs to be let out into the open air on the balcony for a moment, he says a slight case of nausea has befallen him, but it isn't anything serious. Issuing an excuse to the surrounding throng, Stanhope gallantly escorts Kaspar, with exaggerated helpfulness, to the balcony, where he sees that they push him down upon a velvet chair.

Balcony of the ballroom, exterior

Kaspar breathes heavily, freeing himself of his frock coat, he then opens his shirt, which is too tight around his neck. A uniformed man and Daumer are with him. Deadened, dainty conversation from the ballroom, music sets in. The air is doing him good, says Kaspar with a pale face. He should be left in peace for a minute, his sickness is really almost over, says Kaspar to Daumer.

Smaller ballroom, interior

The conversation has shifted to a different subject, as Kaspar's debut is over. The earl, surrounded by distinguished dames, is talking about Corinth and the Sun of Hellas. When he has gotten as far as the horses, an elderly lady laden with jewels steps forth from the side with a knowing glance, tugging at his shirtsleeve for him to come. Stanhope politely excuses himself for a moment and follows the lady. The gaze of the others, suspecting something, follows the couple. They advance towards the balcony.

Balcony of the ballroom, exterior

Stanhope and the lady step outside onto the balcony, where Stanhope remains spellbound with embarrassment. Kaspar is sitting on the velvet chair with his shirt open wide and his sleeves pushed up, sunk into a deep, oblivious abyss, knitting. He holds a little piece of knitting, which he is enlarging. With thick fingers he labors with colossal concentration. The woolen thread with which he knits is winding down to the floor and up again, straight into Kaspar's right pocket. There they perceive the outline of a modest ball of wool.

Stanhope casts a devastating glance at Daumer, who has just entered, and Daumer is pierced by equally-deprecating glances from behind as well. In his indignation, Stanhope leaves no doubt that he is through with Kaspar.

Silence spreads. It is an awful, painful silence, because even the music in the room has ceased. All of this completely escapes Kaspar's attention. He is submerged in his work.

Daumer's garden, beneath the walnut tree.

Daumer and Kaspar are seated together at the table underneath the walnut tree, playing checkers.
Kaspar deliberates before each move with a great
deal of care, positioning the stones in every in-
stance with a cautious inquisitive glance. Katy is
working in the background in a vegetable bed.
After a prolonged silence, Kaspar says it seemed
peculiar, wondering whether Daumer felt it as
well: he felt glances being directed towards him.
He felt glances falling upon him ever so vaguely.
Daumer turns around, reassuring Kaspar that
there is no one in the garden except for Katy.
The feeling was only a vague one, says Kaspar.
Also, an unknown man had spoken to him on
two different days while he was on his way from
the municipal court, and he wondered whether
this had something to do with the renewed police
investigations, or with the fact that someone had
spread some gossip around about his autobio-
graphy. Well, says Daumer, it could be that the
persons who had first hidden and then expelled
him were afraid of his place of confinement being revealed in greater detail. But one also knew
that all investigations into this matter had produced nothing thus far. In the future, by no
means should he walk alone to the municipal
court.

Daumer's house, side view, exterior

The hedge reaches up along this side of the house a few feet. To the rear the garden is open, and towards the front there is a clear view through a high double-winged wooden portal, a small extra entrance has been built in the right wing of the portal. On the side of the house an enclosed staircase made of inlaid wood descends from the second floor. A small improvised outhouse has been built beneath the stairs, closed off from the exterior by a screen. Garden tools and rakes are lying about inside there, as the outhouse is apparently employed by the gardeners. A tiled path runs between the house and the hedge, the rest of the yard is covered by firmly packed sand. In front of the portal, a dog is sleeping in the sun. It is late morning.

Kaspar rounds the house from the garden and tries to enter the house by way of the stairs, but he finds the door locked. He yanks at it once, then turns to the outhouse underneath the stairs without trying any further. When he pushes the screen aside a bit to enter, Katy bends down from a window above and, seeing what the trouble is at once, calls out: "The young gentleman has obviously taken too much of the Welsh nut laxative that the doctor prescribed for him."

Kaspar looks up while closing the screen, leaving it slightly ajar.

Kaspar squats down onto the toilet seat. Through the crack between the screen and the wall of the house, the sleeping dog and part of the portal can be seen. The small door in the portal suddenly opens; we see this only because of the slight movement of the hinges, the rest of the door being obstructed by the screen. The bell above the door jingles softly, and the dog stirs in his sleep.

Kaspar, who obviously hasn't noticed that someone has entered, calls out: "Katy, would you open the door, I think somebody rang." But Katy doesn't come, as she is probably in another room by now.

Behind the screen, Kaspar suddenly holds his breath, aware that someone has already entered. Evidently embarrassed by his situation, he doesn't make a sound.

Through the slits between the joints of the screen, we see from Kaspar's perspective now that someone is approaching hastily, almost silently. The footsteps come to a halt in front of the screen. Kaspar stiffens into a statue of stone, looks under the lower edge of the screen a couple of inches from the ground and sees a pair of boots stop still and move no further. Kaspar doesn't dare breathe.

Someone is standing just as soundlessly in front of the screen. Long breathless tension, extremely tense anticipation. Then an arm rips the screen away with a jerk; Kaspar jumps up and into his pants with a simlar jerk in confused haste. For a split second we recognize the Unknown Man by his clothing, his face veiled by a black kerchief, he lands a blow with a hatchet, as quick as a thought, into the outhouse. Kaspar, hit above the brow, falls forward into the half-open screen. The dog in the background rises, yawns, and

wags his tail as a sound is heard from the house,
The Unknown Man turns away before he can
land a second blow, and flees with silent steps.
The dog stands at the portal, which has remained
open, wagging his tail.

Daumer's house, kitchen

The kitchen door opens, and Daumer sticks his
head in. Katy is arranging pear preserves in the
pantry adjoining the kitchen. Where is Kaspar,
Daumer asks; he hasn't come to his lessons, and
hasn't appeared for lunch at the usual hour,
either. He has already looked in his room. Katy
comes out of the pantry. She had seen him this
morning around a quarter past ten, she answers.

Daumer's house, side

Daumer and Katy are standing by the outhouse,
the screen is completely torn down. Daumer has
discovered a trail of dried blood on the tiles
which reaches past the packed sand to a point
below the hedge, where a lump of dried blood
has gathered in a little hole. Daumer senses evil.

In front of Kaspar's room

In the anteroom of Kaspar's chamber there is a large dark wardrobe. Daumer and Katy are standing in front of it, their faces pale with fright. They have discovered the bloody imprint of a hand.

Entrance to the cellar

Daumer is forcing open a heavy trap door which hides a steep dank staircase leading to the cellar. There, he says, he must have gone down there. On the cellar door we see traces of blood.

In the cellar

It is a frigid gloomy basement room, with walls full of mildew and water dripping to the floor. The entire floor is ankle-deep in water. Kaspar is lying crumpled up in a slightly inclined corner, still conscious. On this one dry spot there are sprouting potatoes as well. Kaspar looks at Daumer and opens his hand. Blood is streaming from his head.

Kaspar's chamber

Kaspar lies in his bed fully clothed, with a make-shift bandage around his forehead. Daumer is supporting his head while Katy puts a bowl of water to his lips, as she was unable to come up with a more suitable drinking vessel in her haste. Kaspar drinks with such fervor that he bites a piece out of the rim. A doctor and a domestic come rushing in through the door.

Kaspar's chamber

Daumer politely ushers the police notary, a scrivener, and a municipal judge out the door from Kaspar's chamber. There is nothing more to get out of Kaspar today, the municipal judge remarks, he really hasn't strength enough yet. Although the patient has made considerable pro-gress in these last few days, he doesn't believe that they can expect any more clues which might lead to a solution of the crime and a clarification of Kaspar's origin. And despite his lingering weakness, he adds, the patient has regained the complete use of his mental faculties, his state-ments are no longer so confused.
Daumer closes the door and turns towards Kas-par, who is reclining in his bed on a pillow, the bandage around his head much smaller. Kaspar is pale and visibly feeble.

164

There is something which has nothing to do with the attack on him says Kaspar, but which he would like to mention anyway, as he was seeing it clearly before him now. He ought to talk about it, Daumer says, if he is sure it won't be too much of a strain.

Vision of the Island

When, in his confusion, he ended up in the cellar instead of the kitchen with Katy, says Kaspar, he sank down unconscious on the only dry spot. Then he very clearly saw a canoe with a man in it rowing in the open sea, he saw the canoe from high above, there were mighty waves. The canoe had reached a rock, like a square pillar in the sea, and atop it was a verdant plateau where he saw a woman with flowing sleeves, who was swinging her sleeves ever so slowly. He knew that this was Death, this woman was Death. Then he looked over the edge of the rock into the sea, he felt drawn into the void, and then the cold water in the cellar brought him back to consciousness. This will not leave his mind.

While Kaspar is speaking we see flickering images. A canoe on massive ocean waves approaches a craggy stone tower. On top of the rocky tower is a sloping plateau, over which fog is floating. There is a low stone wall upon it with strange huts of rough stone running along the edge, huts like igloos made of stone. A woman is standing in the distance wearing a light silk dress and fluttering veils. To her arms she has fastened long floating veils which reach down to the ground. She is swinging her arms slowly and solemnly, like wings. The veils swing like the wings of some majestic bird. The image flickers past. Mist rises from the depths, flowing over the plateau.

Kaspar leans back onto his pillow and grows silent. He is tired now, says Kaspar.

Garden, under the walnut tree

A heavy armchair has been carried from the house over to the walnut tree, beneath which Kaspar usually sits. Kaspar, propped up by a couple of pillows, is sitting there in front of the four parsons. Fuhrmann is seated closest to him once again, but this time Kaspar cannot lean evasively away from him because he is thwarted by the tall back of the chair. It is a warm, sunny day. Kaspar wears a long piece of bandage plastered across his brow.

He cannot imagine that this attempt to murder him had been part of any divine plan, says Kaspar. The screen had somewhat prevented the murderer from landing a solid blow; and it was he, Kaspar himself, who had nailed the screen on one side to the wall because the wind had blown it over several times.

Fuhrmann leans toward him, and since Kaspar cannot back away, he pushes himself subtly up the back of his chair. He should not fret so much about being persecuted, Fuhrmann says, but should place his trust in God instead, for even this murder attempt could not have happened without God's will, nor, he adds, could it have ended so happily.

Kaspar slides slowly down into his normal sitting position. A thought graces his face. Yes, he says, that really makes sense to him; God surely must have something against human beings, judging from the way they were made.

All four pastors begin to talk at once. They hurl a horde of arguments at Kaspar. We can only understand part of what they are saying, something about the wise yet oftentimes inscrutable ways of Divine Reason, of sane suffering for probation, by which we weigh our Faith and abandon ourselves to His will. Otherwise all we know is chaos.

Kaspar sits in his armchair, gazing at the pastors with bewilderment.

Country scene

Kaspar, Daumer and Fuhrmann stand on a small hill overlooking a lovely green valley. A short distance away from the group, a poor old day laborer with an excessively heavy load of wood

167

on his back has paused as well, secretly partaking
in the pleasure of the wayfarers, the gentlemen.
Is this the Labenbach, Fuhrmann wants to know,
this magnificent meadowland! Yes, says the day
laborer, trying not to reveal the stress caused by
the burden on his back, this was the Labenbach;
he works there, he will soon have to mow the
whole meadow, a hard job for just one fellow
like himself.

What a charming, rustic scene this is, and what a
beautiful meadow, Daumer says. Yes, says Fuhrmann, the landscape here is as God commanded
it to be. Kaspar stands off to the side, somewhat
morose, scratching the scar on his forehead.

Daumer turns to him, wanting him to cheer up.
He can't see anything beautiful here, everything
is much too green, says Kaspar. Daumer hands
him a red tinted lens and has him look through
it. Yes, says Kaspar, he likes it this way a little
more, but he still can't call it beautiful since the
children down there — he should turn and look a
bit that way — have such raggedy clothes on
even when he sees them through the red lens.
They surely don't get enough to eat, either.

Daumer leans towards Kaspar a little and, following his gaze, we now see somewhat intimately
an impoverished farmhouse at the bottom of the
hill with some poor-looking children in rags,
barefoot and dirty, who stand stiffly, staring
towards the wayfarers, hesitating in a peculiar
way as if they didn't dare beg from such strangers. They stand there in a weird fearfullness, a
fear that cowers over them.

That, says Fuhrmann, has nothing to do with the landscape, the fertile valley. What is more, he adds, the poor are especially dear to the heart of our Lord.

A poorly-dressed farmer now comes hurrying out of the farmhouse and heads straight towards the three visitors. Even before reaching them he politely begs them to leave. He works this farm with his brother, who is the father of those children. The mother of these poor little urchins died three days ago, and since then his brother was out of his mind with grief. He might be a danger to the gentlemen. Yesterday his brother killed two calves, to show the calves how it feels to lose one's mother.

Daumer and Fuhrmann retreat uncertainly. Kaspar stands rooted to his spot and has to be dragged away by Fuhrmann. The day-laborer transforms into a living monument for all those who must bear too heavy a burden. The rustic scene ensues.

Garden hedge, blackbird nest

Kaspar stands enraptured by the hedge in the farthest corner of the garden. The drenched leaves are dripping with rain, but the rain subsided some time ago. Kaspar cautiously spreads apart a couple of twigs, revealing to us a blackbird's nest in a forked branch about breasthigh containing four young ones who huddle in their nest half-naked still, closely pressing together.

And now we also perceive that Kaspar has pulled a sheer black stocking over his right hand, and that he has made a fist inside underneath. He lets only his middle finger protrude a bit, like a nose. On both sides of the middle finger, where it is attached to the hand, he has stuck two lightly-colored stones, so the fist rather resembles a small face with two eyes and a nose.

Kaspar carefully moves the hand with the tiny face down close to the nest, and to his indescribable delight, the little blackbirds stretch their necks out towards the face, opening their beaks wide while chirping for food. Kaspar withdraws his hand again and lapses into deep thought.

Then he notices that the blackbird mother is sitting with some food on the hedge, very near the nest. Kaspar turns his back quite carefully stepping away stealthily on his heels.

Sunday, square in front of the church

A beautiful, calm, sunny Sunday; on the square in front of the church some sparrows are having a row. Some wagons and carriages nearby. In the background, an old woman is sitting in front of her house on a stone bench, sleeping.

Through the open door of the church we hear the

distant singing of the congregation as services are being held inside. For a long time nothing stirs.

All of a sudden we see Kaspar rushing distractedly out the door and down the steps into the open square, the sparrows take to the air. He wears a black coat with white gloves and looks as if he had been squeezed into his suit. Behind him Daumer hurries down the steps with coattails flying, catching up with Kaspar.

The two of them, closer. Kaspar doesn't even wait for Daumer's question. The congregation's singing seems to him like some repulsive screaming, he says. "First the people scream, and when they leave off, then the parson starts to scream."

Garden, the bed of watercress

Daumer's garden, a calm idyllic spot in the afternoon. Kaspar is sitting under his walnut tree at the little garden table, writing on a big sheet of paper with utter devotion. He dips the pen into a little inkwell, meticulously blowing a wasp away, though it persists in sitting on the edge of his paper. The sun is baking the gooseberry bushes beside him. In the shadow of the bushes, a separate little flower bed has been raked and planted and pruned with a great deal of love. The name KASPAR has been written upon it elegantly with watercress seedlings. Part of the bed is trampled down, with the A and the R having suffered in

171

particular. Kaspar glances up from his sheet of paper, softly reading over to himself what he has written.

Kaspar: "I beg Mr. Daumer to read this paper only with good will. Yesterday it was quiet, so I went in the canoe; and the oarsman sat still, praising the voyage. Days before I had sowed my name with garden cress, and these had come up beautifully, and had caused me so much pleasure that I don't know how to express it. And yesterday, when I come home from the boat trip, there was someone who had entered the garden and borne off with many pears and did trample my name. Then I wept for a long time, and I want to sow the bed anew..."

The light in the garden slowly fades. The stiff trees stand dead still. A music sets in, very gently and devoid of pathos.

Open field, night

It is a bright mild night, the moon is shining over a field and a forest that stands dark and submerged in silence. Kaspar and Daumer are standing with eyes staring upward at the starlit firmament. Kaspar's astonishment and rapture surpass all that we have seen of him so far. This was truly the most beautiful thing he has ever seen in this world, he exclaims. But who was it who put all those many lights up there, who lights them and who puts them out. Daumer tries to explain that the stars, just like the sun which he already knows about, shine all the time, although they aren't always visible.

Again Kaspar asks who it was who put them up there so that they are burning all the time. And why can't one see them during the day, where are they then. Finally, with head bowed, he sinks into deep serious thought.

Kaspar sets himself on a bench and asks Daumer why that evil man had kept him locked in all the time without ever letting him see any of these wonderful things. He wished that someone would put this man in prison, too, for just one day, so that he knew what it meant to be in Darkness. After that, Kaspar lapses into prolonged weeping that can hardly be stopped. Daumer stands still and does not know how to help him.

Daumer's garden, gravel path

Daumer is walking along the garden path lost in thought, a book tucked under his arm. Katy is pulling weeds from a vegetable bed.

Kaspar suddenly rushes towards him, tottering and stopping in front of Daumer. Like a mime on the stage, he mutely holds his arms outstretched and flails about frightfully.

For God's sake what has happened to him, says

Daumer, who discovers blood and a puncture wound in Kaspar's breast. Katy rushes over from her bed with her fingers full of mud. Kaspar cannot speak. He tries to pull Daumer with him.

In the Hofgarten

Kaspar is pulling Daumer with him across a lawn in the park. He stumbles rather than walks.

Hofgarten, small fountain

A small stone fountain with some nymphs. Behind it an artificial, ivy-covered grotto. The fountain has dried up and the muddy ground nearby has been excavated into a pit. Evidently they are repairing the water pipes, but there aren't any workmen. A few shovels and pushcarts are scattered around. Huge chestnut trees in the background.
We see Kaspar pulling Daumer towards the fountain. He stops near the pit and points to the ground. That, there, was given to him by the man who then stabbed him. Kaspar suddenly regains his speech.
Closer. We see a small black bag on the ground,

which is now picked up by Daumer. It seems to be empty, but then a small piece of paper folded over several times emerges.

The slip of paper, close up; backwards script to be read reflected in a mirror. We hear Kaspar blurt out that the park gardener had ordered him here by a messenger, to see the various levels of earth at the excavation.

Daumer, who has realized that the strange symbols on the paper are mirror-script, holds the paper against the sun so he can see the text show through on the other side. He reads: "Hauser will be able to tell you what I look like and where I am from. To save Hauser the trouble I shall tell you myself where I come from...I come from the Bayvarian border...at the river... I even want to tell you my name—M.L. O...

Daumer's house, entrance

Mrs. Hiltel runs up to the entrance and rings. The door is opened at once from within.

Kaspar's room

Kaspar is half-reclining on the bed, pale and disfigured, an image of horror. He hasn't removed his clothes yet, on his chest alone the clothes and the shirt have been pulled apart. Kaspar is not completely stretched out, his body turned to the wall in a half-lying, half-sitting position, his legs dangling from the bed onto the floor.

Daumer is in the room and Katy hands him a bowl with a damp cloth. Fuhrman has squeezed himself in beside the bed, trying to stay out of the way. The surgeon-general of the town is with Kaspar, fondling his wound, which is not visible to us because of Kaspar's half-averted position. Mrs. Hiltel comes into the room.

"Mother shall come, Mother shall come, the Mother," whispers Kaspar, but he doesn't recognize Mrs. Hiltel, who is bending over him. The doctor raises Kaspar's upper torso, bending him forward a bit, then he feels with his little finger down in the wound. He can feel a membrane, he says, and now he distinctly feels the throbbing heart mucscle with his fingertip. The wound now seems more dangerous than it had appeared to be from the surface. "To Regensburg, to Regensburg," Kaspar calls out, and in his delirium he springs halfway out of bed. The doctor is still sticking his finger into Kaspar's breast, wrestling him down again with a great deal of effort. Kaspar loses consciousness.

Daumer's living room

On his sofa, which has been converted to a bed,
Kaspar lies in a yellow jaundiced pallor, though
inwardly he is serene. The room is filled with
people, and from the appearance of those surrounding Kaspar's bed we can gather that this is
his deathbed. Mrs. Hiltel is present with Julius, a
doctor, a male nurse, Daumer, Katy, the
municipal judge, Fuhrmann, and the three
pastors. Embarrassed stillness reigns. Kaspar is
clearly conscious but only manages to whisper.
The people stand solemnly around Kaspar's bed.
Do you have anything to relieve your heart of,
Fuhrmann says, bending over. Yes, says Kaspar
and stays silent. Then, after a long pause: there
was the story of the desert, of the caravan, but
he still knew just the beginning of it. He should
tell it anyway, says Daumer, that wouldn't matter now.

Vision of the Sahara

Kaspar, close. He is silent again. After awhile he
begins to whisper. He saw a long caravan coming
through the desert. In the caravan were merchants, and suddenly some of them were puzzled
because the outline of some hazy mountains was
emerging before them. One of them now rode up

ahead to stop the leader. They seemed to have lost their way as tall mountains appeared in front of them, they were beholding towering mountains. There the blind leader stopped, sniffed the wind and then took a handful of sand from the ground, tasting it carefully. Son, says the blind man, son, you are wrong. What you see before you are not mountains. It was just an hallucination, it was just a mirage. They headed further north. Yes, they headed irrevocably northward, and then the real story began, in some oriental city. The story should be called: City in the Mountains, or, City of the Far North, but the history that transpired in this city he didn't know.

While Kaspar narrates, images are flickering past. We see a big caravan like errant light come over the sand dunes, mythically grand. We see the blind Berber, walking in front on foot. We see fat Arabian merchants, pointing ahead, scanning a map, reading a compass with confused gestures. We see a fat merchant driving a dromedary forward. We see how he dismounts, stopping the leader. We see glimmering mountains swimming as if in a lake. The leader tastes the sand with his tongue like a cook. The images become lighter, flickering away.

Kaspar, close. He has reflected for quite some time, Kaspar whispers, but the actual story has not occurred to him yet. He is silent for a long while. He thanks them for listening to him. He is tired, says Kaspar.

In the Anatomy

A bare room: the anatomy chamber, a tiled floor which inclines from all sides towards a drain in the room. Big, high windows; from outside the light heats within. On one of the side walls a faucet without a sink, which is fully flowing constantly though no one closes it. The water runs into a drain beside the table. On the table is Kaspar's corpse, whitish, with yellow-green patches; the body is opened wide and pulled apart with hooks. The head is nearly beyond recognition because the top of the skull has been removed and the brain set free.

Close. On the sole of Kaspar's foot is a simple registration tag adhering to it with glue, with the initials K.H., a date, and some elaborate registration numbers.

Five physicians are leaning over Kaspar's corpse, disemboweling him like vultures. Quiet, busy, matter-of-fact, scientific greed.

"Mister Surgeon-General," one of them says, "Look, there you are, the liver, the left lobe in particular is stretching extremely far, swollen all the way to the pleura." "I cannot see," says the Surgeon-General, pushing in front, "Mr. Physician, please remove this exudation first so I can judge for myself."

The interest intensifies, they have discovered something abnormal, as if that could explain everything. After having separated the two hemispheres of the brain, one of them discovers that the cerebellum is rather large and well-developed in relation to the cerebrum, and that the posterior lobe of the left hemisphere refuses to cover the cerebellum, as is normally the case. The busy greed increases as something extraordinary has been discovered, the brain is being sliced into pieces. From the tap the water keeps flowing full force, the light from the window is blinding.

Then, all of a sudden, music sets in. An aria from a very old recording, full of dignity, beautiful and solemn. The voice carries peacefully and without strain. The doctors work efficiently, diabolically. The water flows incessantly from the faucet. The music overwhelms the conversation.

Then, as the music grows stronger, our gaze moves slowly away from the group and is drawn as if by magic to the window. The light becomes painfully bright. View from the window; outside on a dusty square, blinding as if lighted by electricity, three people are standing immobile. They are waiting. Then after a long time, the carriage they have been waiting for arrives. It emerges swiftly from trees that are petrified from the heat. White, glowing dust swirls up and settles again, glaringly hot. The carriage stops right in front of the people. Calmly and as a matter of course, the coachman waits until the three have entered the open carriage. All available seats are taken. Now we expect the carriage to leave as matter-of-factly as it arrived, but it simply doesn't move. No stirring, no protest from the passengers. They just sit there like stone, and the vehicle doesn't move. Why aren't they moving, the carriage had come so swiftly. Prolonged stasis, nothing stirs, the passengers sit, staring straight ahead.

A stray dog passing by increases the lifeless rigidity. The horse, playing with its ears apathetically,
slowly lowers its head.

The music stops. A gruesome horrible light over
everything, without shadows. The carriage stands
and stands and doesn't move on. In the midst of
this unheard-of rigidity and paralysis, the vehicle
stands stock-still with the people inside it. The
square is filled with electric inflexibility.

The carriage doesn't, and doesn't, and doesn't
move on.

Dialogue from:

Land of Silence and Darkness

"From the life of the deaf and blind Fini Straubinger"

Darkness, Quietude

The Field Path

Fini Straubinger: I see before me a path that leads across an unplowed field, and fugitive clouds fleeing past.

The Ski-Jumper

As a child, when I could still see and hear, I once visited a ski-jumping event; and this image keeps returning to my mind, how these men were hovering in the air. I watched their faces very closely. I wish you could see that too, once.

On the Park Bench

Resi Mittermeier: Could Mrs. Straubinger tell us about the animals again?

Fini: That was such an enormous pleasure for us. First we were led into the room for the crawling animals. There was a roebuck of normal size — they were all normal animals that had been stuffed for the instruction of the blind. There was a very beautiful roebuck, its fur was so beautiful. Beside it lay a stag's head of a capital buck, a twelve-branched antler. And there was its neck as well, and the gaping mouth. I was awestruck by that huge animal. Then there were — hares, yes! — in leaping and sitting posture, one could touch them all over. Some of us felt creepy because there were also some mice. In the second room there were only the flying animals. First there was a black woodpecker on a branch, which was interesting. . . then its little brother, the colored woodpecker. I was enraptured! Those long beaks! Then a pheasant with its long feathers. What a pity that we couldn't see the colors.

Resi: Could Miss Julie tell us about the animals as well?

Fini: They are asking you whether you can talk about the animals.

Julie: I don't remember much.

Fini: She doesn't remember much. But, what you do remember.

Julie: I touched some animals that I had never seen before in my life — pheasants, crocodiles, snakes, tigers, lions, and several others. And some which we also have here in Europe — goats, roebucks, hares, foxes, and even a mouse.

On the Plane
Title: Flying for the first time
Photos
Title: Memories
In Fini's Room

Fini: As a child I was very tempermental. My mother had a hard time with me and tried time and time again to keep me in line. Father died at the age of thirty-three, I wasn't even six years old. And so it happened that I lived my own life whenever I had the slightest breath of fresh air. Then it came to pass that I fell down the stairs at the age of nine. That is to say, I somersaulted from the third floor down to the second, and I fell so hard on my back and on the back of my head that a man who was standing nearby thought it was a gunshot. He asked: Did you hurt yourself? No, I said. Please, don't tell Mommy or else she will spank me. And on all fours I crept up the stairs, for I couldn't walk any more. Apparently I was very frightened and had received quite a shock. . . like a good child I sat down beneath the window and pleaded: Holy guardian angel help so Mommy doesn't spank me! But from then on I always had nausea and headaches, something I had never known before. When the vomiting started, the doctor thought it was from growing, the second one said the same. Only the third doctor said that the child had suffered a fall. And at school I was very attentive and I showed interest — the schoolmistress said one day: Listen Fini, you must pay attention not to write below the line! Yes, I said, but I always pay attention. Then it occurred to me that I didn't even see the line. I had wanted to embroider very much, and then it happened that I was forced to stop half-way through my embroidery. The teacher said: Go home, you can't see it anyway. And I didn't feel like knitting. . . but. And from then on, it gradually went downhill. First, I went totally blind at the

age of fifteen and three-quarters. At that
time I also had to stay in bed, I had some
very serious inflammations of the eyes. And
then at the age of eighteen my hearing began
to fail me. At first I didn't realize what that
funny buzzing in my ears was. And then one
day I simply didn't hear anymore. Mother
spoke to me and I didn't understand her.
She came to my bed and said: But don't you
hear me? Why don't you answer? I asked:
What? Did you say something? Yes, of
course, she said. I talked to you all that
time, and you have given no answer. So I
said: But Mommy I didn't hear you. Then
we both were very frightened. And it kept
changing: sometimes I didn't hear with my
right ear, and sometimes I didn't hear with
my left. I wanted to see a doctor, I wanted
help, I tried foot baths, I prayed fervently,
but it didn't help. Gradually I proceeded to
lose my hearing, down to five percent. In-
itially I accepted it from the religious side.
That gave me strength, but the loneliness,
the terrible loneliness stayed with me. People
promised: Yes, I will come and visit you,
but they didn't come; and if they ever did,
they sat at my bedside chatting with my
mother, and I was very quiet. And when I
asked, I received a slight tap, and: Be quiet,
I'll tell you later what we were talking
about. Yes, I wanted to grasp something of
life.

Resi: How long were you confined to the bed?

Fini: Almost thirty years. Again and again I tried to get up. There were periods when I could hardly move. Were those ever times! Then the doctor realized that it was a permanent disease, that perhaps it would take a very long time, and he deprived me of the morphine. That was hard for me, but I got over it. It is like this: One thinks of deafness, that it is complete stillness. But Oh no, that is wrong. It is a never-ending noise in the head, ranging down to the lowest ringing, perhaps the way sand sounds, trickling, then knocking, but worst of all it pounds in the head so that one never knows where to turn one's head. That is a great torture for us. This is the reason why we are sometimes so touchy, and don't know what to do. It is precisely the same thing with blindness: It is not complete darkness. Oftentimes there are very strange shades of color in front of one's eyes: black, gray, white, blue, green, yellow. . . it depends.

Birthday Party

Fini: Hello, Mr. Messmer! I'm so pleased that you've come.
Commentary: On her 56th birthday, Fini Straubinger has invited friends who are, just

like her, deaf and blind at the same time.
Such a party is not easy to organize because
each deaf and blind person needs a helper
who interprets the conversation into his
hand, for amongst themselves they can neither see nor hear.

Hello, hello, Mrs. Meier, Mr. Forster, where
is Mr. Forster? Hello, Mr. Forster! Please
tell Mrs. Meier what we are talking about.
That is someone with remnants of eyesight.
But this group must be looked after as well
so that they are not pushed overnight into
the Land of Silence and Darkness. Hello,
dear little Julie.

Julie: Where is Mr. Hundhammer?

Fini: O noble knight George, where are you?
Here! Good afternoon, Mr. Hundhammer. I
am sincerely grateful that you will be looking after Julie. Good afternoon!

Julie: Has everyone arrived?

Mr. Hundhammer: Yes. Yes, they are all there.

Fini: Who, but who is this? Mrs. Augustin?
No. . . that's Chipmunk! Welcome, my
Chipmunk!

To all people present, a nice afternoon!
Now please, who can recite a poem?

Julie: I would like to ask that you translate for
the deaf and blind in the finger alphabet. I
shall speak as slowly as possible so that the
people can keep up with me. For when the
deaf and blind forever squats down, staring
into the void, he feels ever so oppressed,
and now I am going to read a poem which is

particularly suited for this point in time. It
is entitled: "The Finest Art".
To see from afar, how others rejoice,
fills with pleasure the holiest task,
and for our own good nothing do we ask,
To live in the shade, the sun so far,
and yet to shine, for the others a star,
that is an art, which only he knows,
In whose soul the wind of heaven blows.
Deaf and blind woman: Shall I begin? Yes.
Annie with her pretty hood
is at all times kind and good.
Dost for our care and keep
every day our staircase sweep.
Our thanks do we convey,
here and now, and every day.

Botanical Garden

Commentary: In the afternoon, Fini Straubinger
and her guests visit the botanical garden.
Gardener: You may touch one if you like, be-
cause they are very solid. Pillar-shaped. . .
Resi: Pillar-shaped. Nothing but cactus!
Gardener: Yes.
Fini: How interesting!
Gardener: Here we come to the fruits of the cac-
tus. . .
Resi: A fruit of a cactus. . .

Gardener: We might as well pick one. This is the
    fruit.
    The natives eat it, its meat. . . (is quite frui-
    ty)
Fini: Who can eat that?
Gardener: The natives.
Resi: The natives.
Fini: Are they ripe yet?
Gardener: No, not like that.
Fini: Thank you.
Gardener: No, not like that.
Fini: Thank you.
Gardener: You are welcome.
Fini: Look here. . . A bamboo!
Resi: This is a bamboo, isn't it?
Herzog: No!
Fini: Look here, I imagined it to be quite dif-
    ferent. . .

On the Train

Fini: All of that will be in January. . . then again
    we will have a lot of work. First of all the
    visits here, then the trip to the Upper Pala-
    tinate. No, before Christmas is out of the
    question! I wonder just how much I will
    have to prepare for Christmas. . .Mr.
    Schwarzhuber said I should prepare a play.
    But how, what, and when?

Commentary: For four years, Fini Straubinger has been taking care of the deaf and blind people in Bavaria. She was nominated to do so by the Bavarian Association for the Blind. With her companion Resi Mittermeier, who guides her and interprets by a finger alphabet, she makes regular visiting tours in the country. She establishes contact with the deaf and blind there, taking care of their problems.

Ah, my ticket, thank you!
If I were endowed with the divine gift of a painter, I would paint the fate of the deaf and blind roughly like this: Blindness as a dark melodious stream which slowly but surely flows towards a fall. To the left and to the right are beautiful trees with flowers and birds which sing wonderfully. The other stream, which comes from the other side, should be very clear and transparent. This stream flows slowly and soundlessly downward as well, and then, below, there is a very dark, deep lake. First there would be rocks on both sides where the rivers converge, the dark one and the clear one, against which the waters push, foam and form whirlpools; and then, very slowly, very very very gently, they flow together in this very dark pool. And these waters would be very still and from time to time they would spray upward. This would depict the tortured soul of the deaf and blind. I don't know if you actually understood properly. The pushing and spraying of the waters a-

gainst the rock are, so to speak, the psychological depressions of the soul which accompany the deaf and blind when he proceeds towards deafness and blindness. I cannot paint it otherwise, it is right inside me so, but one doesn't know to get it out in words.

In the Insane Asylum

Commentary: Here in a Lower Bavarian asylum, Else Fehrer has been living for two years; she is forty-eight years old. Her mother, the only person with whom she could communicate, is dead.

Fini: Welcome, my dear companion of Fate! Yes, that is the sign of recognition. Miss Fehrer attended the School for the Blind in Munich for two years as a child. She learned braille, but since she has had no practice she has forgotten.

Commentary: Since no charity or old people's home would accept Else Fehrer, she was sent, out of necessity, to an insane asylum, where she doesn't belong at all. Else Fehrer withdrew completely into herself. She never spoke again.

Fini: The last years that she spent with her mother she was still able to read somewhat from the mouth. But that is over now as well.

Resi Mittermeier: She is looking at me all the time.

Fini: Ah, well. . .
       For you, my dear Else, yes, for you.

Resi: She's looking at you all the time.

Fini: I. . . blind. . . deaf, like you, blind and deaf, too. Not another word more.

Resi: No.

Fini: I might try. . . (guides Else's hand in cursive letters) blind... deaf, yes! You and I are sisters of Fate! You poor, poor human being, no contact with the world!

Resi: She doesn't speak.

Fini: Yes, it is because she has forgotten her speech over these many years. There is no bridge to her.

Resi: Fini — Fini Straubinger, from Munich, yes?

Fini: Does she speak?

Resi: No. But she is looking at us attentively.

Title: When you let go of my hand it is as if we were separated by a thousand miles.

Congress Hall

German President Heinemann: The other group of those who cannot cope with an achievement oriented society, which literally means: those who cannot GET their right if it is only the achievement that counts, are the handicapped. To them society owes more than tolerance for what they are, or how they are. To them society owes a taking into its midst in myriad ways. Ultimately, we deal

194

with the consciousness of us all in our attitude towards handicapped people. And I must speak out at this point in utter frankness that I consider some of our attitudes in our society, I consider them terrifying. A society which doesn't know how to treat old people, sick people and handicapped people of all kinds as a natural part of its own, proclaims its own judgement.

On the Park Bench

Fini: That was a very great experience. Yes, I was quite taken aback when the president first approached me and grabbed my left hand with his left hand. His hand was cool, but not cold. And as I was presenting my petition I kept feeling a slight pressure, so that I knew I was understood, and that I was truly understood. And what I said was the following:
Honorable Mr. President! Please grant your benign attention to the deaf and blind as well. Help us out of our isolation. . . help us to find noble people who will lift us out of our loneliness.

Resi: Could you explain to us how "Lorming" works?

Fini: Oh yes! The entire Lorming system consists of strokes and points. But one must watch very closely how to apply the points and strokes. For example: The short strokes are made from top to bottom: h, g, d, b, and p from bottom to top. Q is this, the a, e, i, o, u is tapped on the fingertips. If you tap with all of your four fingers into the palm of the hand, it is a k. If you make a stroke across the palm of the hand, it is a z. And the entire alphabet is like this.

Farmhouse

Fini: R, e, Pleasure.
Ursula: Yes. I takes a long time, doesn't it, until I understand.
Resi: Who practices with you sometimes?
Ursula: How, with me? Lorming? No one. Like my brother says: Don't reckon I can recall.
Resi: Then you could talk to him more easily.
Ursula: Naw, he only follows the dialect.
Commentary: On a farm near Freising, Fini Straubinger visits the brother and sister, Ursula and Joseph Rittermeier. She is deaf and almost blind, but she can still understand language by reading lips.
Ursula:: You only follow dialect. You can't speak High German, no.
Commentary: Her brother is blind, though he still possesses remnants of hearing.
Ursula: Lorming, you said, you'll never learn. Can't follow it, you said.

Resi: He has said Straubinger.

Fini: I have brought you a money box.

Ursula: Here, look!

Fini: Joseph, I have brought your money box.

Ursula: You can put in ten pfennig pieces, five pfennigs, one mark, fifty pfennigs. . . Now stick it in, uh-huh, an' when you need it, shove it through again, then the money will pop out. Don't shove too hard! Thataway! Got it? Okay? Now shove it in. Naw, press first. Naw, not yet.

This is our parents' house. And this is our vegetable garden. And there is the meadow. There my brother Joseph often mowed with his scythe.

Ursula: The laundry, yes.

Fini: A big wash, mmm.

Joseph, I don't see or hear either, just like you. We are comrades in Fate. . . but now I'm wobbly.

Resi: Ask him if he understood.

Ursula: You get that?

Joseph: Yes.

Ursula: Your head, man! Stand up, Sepp, you ain't so old yet.

Zoo

Commentary: These deaf and blind here have never been to the zoo. Some of them have not touched a live animal in years. It would be simple to provide them with such a pleasure, but you find too few people who are willing to guide deaf and blind people.

Fini (with chimpanzee): Shall I let go? We must not hurt him! There now, good.

Fini (with a little goat): May I pick it up? But only if the mother approves. . .

Zoo Director: Yes, yes.

Hannover School for the Deaf and Blind
Title: Children born deaf and blind

Mr. Baske: This is Harold, Mrs. Straubinger. Harold is one of my first pupils, he came to me five years ago. He came as a small untamed boy, upsetting everything and breaking everything. It took a lot of effort to make him adjust to a daily routine, to familiarize him with his duties. It took a year for him to grasp the preliminary concept of the finger alphabet. Helen Keller speaks of this grasping as the recognition, the spiritual birth of the deaf and blind. And thus, the actual schooling for deaf and blind children commences at this moment. Since Michael, who sits next to me, still had remnants of hearing, we did not start him on the finger alphabet, but we have used on him the vibration method developed by the

Americans, in which the children feel the word from the lips and repeat it. Michael, this is a car with a trailer! It is very difficult to guess the mood of our pupils, their thoughts and their emotions, and in most cases we are forced to resort to our own supposition.

Fini: I can still remember being there two and a half years ago, when Harold was such a young foal, so to speak. He was inclined towards watches and bracelets.

Mr. Baske: It is much more difficult to teach them abstract terms. We dress up these abstract terms in little stories: If we explain "good", "loving", we say: Harold gets up, Harold studies, Harold helps Sabina, Harold is good. Then we try to classify the opposite by saying: Harold spanks Sabina, Harold pulls Sabina's hair, Harold snatches something from Sabina, Harold is bad. Thus, with a little example, you can demonstrate how we explain "good" and "bad".

Swimming Pool

Baske: So, Mrs. Straubinger, now we will dip into the water. . .

Commentary: Harold was scared to death by the water. It has taken over a year to get him to follow his teacher into the swimming pool.

Baske: And now I am trying to make him wade
through the pool alone.

School

Mistress: Au-
Pupil: Au-
Mistress: -to, -to
Pupil: -to, -to. . .
Mistress: Yes! Michael also says "Auto"
Michael: Auto.
Mistress: Once more come here! Yes, speak up!
Michael: Auto.
Mistress: The lamp is also blue. La-
Commentary: During the language lessons ear-
phones are used as well. Harold can feel the
sound waves through the vibrations. But even if
these children learn to speak in entire sentences,
it is still almost impossible to teach them abstract
terms. What they really imagine by "ambition",
"hope", or "happiness" will forever be alien to
us.

Apartment, Waldkraiburg

Commentary: Vladimir Kokol is 22 years old and was born deaf and blind. All his life he has been taken care of by his father exclusively, and he has never had special training. His needs have never been used in order to stimulate his learning. No one has ever tried to awaken his sense of Reason. Vladimir has never learned to walk properly, he almost always accepts soft food which he gnashes with his tongue against his palate.

Fini: There he is! Welcome, Vladimir! I am just showing him so he knows that someone is there.

With patience and observation you can still get a lot out of him. He certainly won't learn how to talk any more, but I am sure he will learn to interpret gestures. Something I've been observing from time to time is that he presses his nails into my hand, but that is merely because he can't make himself understood otherwise. I am certain this isn't malicious. Don't scratch, my little one! Now look, now he is giving me the other hand!

This is a radio, isn't it? He loves that, because he feels something alive. Is this music? How do you put him to bed?

Father: Just guide him in front of the bed, then he goes.

Fini: Can he keep to the day and night rhythm at all? For that is often very difficult with the deaf and blind. They simply cannot keep to the day and night rhythm.

Resi: Does he know when it's day and when it's night, when one gets up and when one goes to bed. . .

Father: No, he doesn't know at all, but when it is time to sleep, then someone has to lead him to the bed.

Resi: But then is he really willing to go to bed?

Father: Yes.

Resi: He can't dress and undress alone?

Father: No he can't.

Fini: Ah, look, I've observed something!
(Vladimir crosses himself)
I must talk as well. I am sure you can get a lot out of him. Be good! Now he is getting bored. Yes, I think so, too.

Old Age Home, Autumnal Park

Commentary: For five years, Heinrich Fleischmann, 51 years old, has been living with his mother in an old folk's home near Noerdlingen. At the age of thirty-five, the farmer's son went blind on top of his congenital deafness. From then on his relatives neglected him so that he completely forgot how to read and write. After being expelled from the human community, Heinrich Fleischmann sought the companionship of animals. For years he has lived with cattle in a barn.

Mother: He is seeking your hand, don't you see?

Resi: He is seeking the mother's hand.

Mother: He only knows me from my ring.

Fini: We want to chat.

Resi and Fini: Can he talk?

Mother: Yes, if he could read lips he could speak everything. I could talk with him when he was still able to read lips, when he was still able to see. But five years ago, for example, during the winter, I led him to the window, and he said, "Snow." But I can't bring anything close to him.

Resi: Now and then a word. . .

Mother: Very seldom, very seldom!

Resi: And when we were here, did he afterwards ask who it was, or not?

Mother: No. . .

Mother: Nothing, nothing. When my children come, he recognizes none of them.

Resi: He doesn't know his own brothers and sisters anymore?

Mother: No, he doesn't know who it is.

Resi: He doesn't want any more strangers.

Fini: He must have had his experiences. . .

Mother: Oh, there is bound to be a lot that I don't know about.

Fini: Goodbye.

Mother: Ah, Heinrich, he is escaping now.

Resi: Did you say goodbye to him?

Fini: Yes, I did say goodbye to him. Goodbye, Mrs. Fleischmann. All the best for the coming year as well! Goodbye!

Mother (to the camera): Goodbye, gentleman!

Written Title: If a World War broke out now, I wouldn't even notice it.

Werner Herzog was born in 1942 in Munich, Germany. Since 1962, he has been making short films and feature films of his own production. The films, *Last Words (1967)*, *Signs of Life (1968)*, *Precautions Against Fanatics (1969)*, *Land of Silence and Darkness (1971)*, *Aguirre, the Wrath of God (1973)*, *The Great Ectasy of Sculptor Steiner (1975)*, *Heart of Glass (1976)*, *How Much Wood Can a Woodchuck Chuck (1977)*, *La Soufriere (1977)* and *Woyzeck (1979)* are available for rental from New Yorker Films, 16 West 61st Street, New York 10023.